TURNING POINTS

Preparing American Youth for the 21st Century

THE REPORT OF THE TASK FORCE
ON EDUCATION OF YOUNG ADOLESCENTS

CARNEGIE COUNCIL ON ADOLESCENT DEVELOPMENT
CARNEGIE CORPORATION OF NEW YORK
JUNE 1989

Ordering information

Single copies of the **full report** may be obtained for $9.95. Bulk rates for the full report are: 11–25 copies: $8.95 each; 26–99: $6.95; 100–499: $5; 500+: $4; bookstore rate: $6. Single and multiple copies of the **abridged version** of *Turning Points* are available free of charge. Either version may be ordered from Carnegie Corporation of New York, P.O. Box 753, Waldorf, MD 20604. Telephone: (800) 998-2269. Fax: (301) 843-0159. E-mail: ccny@tasco1.com

Prepayment is required. Checks or money orders should be made payable to Carnegie Corporation of New York. Credit card and purchase orders will not be accepted.

Further information

A listing of all Carnegie Council on Adolescent Development publications is available from Carnegie Corporation of New York, 437 Madison Avenue, New York, NY 10022, or on the Internet by accessing http://www.carnegie.org on the World Wide Web. Telephone: (212) 207-6321. Fax: (212) 754-4073.

Library of Congress Cataloging-in-Publication Data

Carnegie Council on Adolescent Development. Task Force on Education of Young Adolescents.

    Turning points: Preparing American youth for the 21st century: the report of the Task Force on Education of Young Adolescents.

    p.   cm.
    "June 1989."
    Bibliography: p.
    ISBN 0–9623154–1–9: $9.95
    1. Middle schools — United States.   2. Junior high school students — United States.   3. Youth — United States — Social conditions.   4. Youth — Health and hygiene — United States.   I. Title.

LB1623.C27 1989   89–15752
373.18'0973 — dc20   CIP

Reprinted July 1998 and October 1999
Designed by Meadows Design Office, Inc., Washington, D.C.
www.mdomedia.com

Edited by Joseph Foote

Cover illustration by Jill Ryerson, Age 11, 6th Grade, Georgetown Day School, Washington, D.C. / Susan Bushee, Teacher

David W. Hornbeck

Bill Clinton

James P. Comer

Alonzo A. Crim

Jacquelynne Eccles

Lawrence W. Green

Fred M. Hechinger

Renee R. Jenkins

Nancy L. Kassebaum

Hernan LaFontaine

Deborah W. Meier

Amado Padilla

Anne C. Petersen

Jane Quinn

Mary Budd Rowe

Roberta G. Simmons

Marshall S. Smith

YOUNG ADOLESCENTS FACE SIGNIF-
icant turning points. For many youth 10 to 15 years old, early adolescence
offers opportunities to choose a path toward a productive and fulfilling life.
For many others, it represents their last best chance to avoid a diminished
future.

Early adolescence is characterized by significant growth and change.
For most, the period is initiated by puberty, a period of development more
rapid than in any other phase of life except infancy. Cognitive growth is
equally dramatic for many youth, bringing the new capacity to think in
more abstract and complex ways than they could as children. Increased
sense of self and enhanced capacity for intimate relationships can also
emerge in early adolescence. All of these changes represent significant
potential in our young people and great opportunity for them and the
society.

Unfortunately, by age 15, substantial numbers of American youth are
at risk of reaching adulthood unable to meet adequately the requirements
of the workplace, the commitments of relationships in families and with
friends, and the responsibilities of participation in a democratic society.
These youth are among the estimated 7 million young people — one in
four adolescents — who are extremely vulnerable to multiple high-risk behaviors and school failure. Another 7 million may be at moderate risk, but
remain a cause for serious concern.

During early adolescence, youth enter a period of trial and error
during which many first experiment with alcohol and drugs and risk
permanent addiction. More and more adolescents 15 years old and
younger are becoming sexually active, risking sexually transmitted
diseases or pregnancy and the birth of unhealthy, low-birthweight babies.

The conditions of early adolescence have changed dramatically from
previous generations. Today, young people enter a society that at once
denounces and glorifies sexual promiscuity and the use of illicit drugs.
They live in urban neighborhoods and even in some rural towns where the
stability of close-knit relationships is rare, where the sense of community
that shapes their identity has eroded. They will seek jobs in an economy
that will require virtually all workers to think flexibly and creatively as
only an elite few were required, and educated, to do in the past.

In these changed times, when young people face unprecedented
choices and pressures, all too often the guidance they needed as children
and need no less as adolescents is withdrawn. Freed from the dependency
of childhood, but not yet able to find their own path to adulthood, many
young people feel a desperate sense of isolation. Surrounded only by their
equally confused peers, too many make poor decisions with harmful or
lethal consequences.

Middle grade schools — junior high, intermediate, and middle schools
— are potentially society's most powerful force to recapture millions of
youth adrift, and help every young person thrive during early adolescence. Yet all too often these schools exacerbate the problems of young
adolescents.

A volatile mismatch exists between the organization and curriculum
of middle grade schools and the intellectual and emotional needs of young

adolescents. Caught in a vortex of changing demands, the engagement of many youth in learning diminishes, and their rates of alienation, substance abuse, absenteeism, and dropping out of school begin to rise.

As the number of youth left behind grows, and opportunities in the economy for poorly educated workers diminish, we face the specter of a divided society: one affluent and well-educated, the other poorer and ill-educated. We face an America at odds with itself.

THE RECOMMENDATIONS CONTAINED in this report will vastly improve the educational experiences of all middle grade students, but will most benefit those at risk of being left behind. The Task Force calls for middle grade schools that:

▲ *Create small communities for learning* where stable, close, mutually respectful relationships with adults and peers are considered fundamental for intellectual development and personal growth. The key elements of these communities are schools-within-schools or houses, students and teachers grouped together as teams, and small group advisories that ensure that every student is known well by at least one adult.

▲ *Teach a core academic program* that results in students who are literate, including in the sciences, and who know how to think critically, lead a healthy life, behave ethically, and assume the responsibilities of citizenship in a pluralistic society. Youth service to promote values for citizenship is an essential part of the core academic program.

▲ *Ensure success for all students* through elimination of tracking by achievement level and promotion of cooperative learning, flexibility in arranging instructional time, and adequate resources (time, space, equipment, and materials) for teachers.

▲ *Empower teachers and administrators to make decisions about the experiences of middle grade students* through creative control by teachers over the instructional program linked to greater responsibilities for students' performance, governance committees that assist the principal in designing and coordinating school-wide programs, and autonomy and leadership within sub-schools or houses to create environments tailored to enhance the intellectual and emotional development of all youth.

▲ *Staff middle grade schools with teachers who are expert at teaching young adolescents* and who have been specially prepared for assignment to the middle grades.

▲ *Improve academic performance through fostering the health and fitness* of young adolescents, by providing a health coordinator in every middle grade school, access to health care and counseling services, and a health-promoting school environment.

▲ *Reengage families in the education of young adolescents* by giving families meaningful roles in school governance, communicating with families about the school program and student's progress, and offering families opportunities to support the learning process at home and at the school.

▲ *Connect schools with communities,* which together share responsibility for each middle grade student's success, through identifying service opportunities in the community, establishing partnerships and collaborations to ensure students' access to health and social services, and using community resources to enrich the instructional program and opportunities for constructive after-school activities.

THE EARLY ADOLESCENT YEARS ARE crucial in determining the future success or failure of millions of American youth. All sectors of the society must be mobilized to build a national consensus to make transformation of middle grade schools a reality. The Task Force calls upon all sectors that care about youth to form partnerships that will create for young adolescents a time of purposeful exploration and preparation for constructive adulthood.

The Task Force calls upon the education sector to start changing middle grade schools now. Teachers and principals are at the center of this process. We urge superintendents and boards of education to give teachers and principals the authority to make essential changes, and work collaboratively to evaluate student outcomes effectively.

We ask leaders in higher education to focus immediately on changes needed in the preparation of middle grade teachers and in ways of collaborating with middle schools to support their reform.

We urge health educators and health care professionals to join with schools to ensure students' access to needed services and to the knowledge and skills that can prevent health-damaging behaviors.

We call upon youth-serving and community organizations, many with significant experience in working with young adolescents, to develop or strengthen their partnerships with middle grade schools.

We call upon states to convene statewide task forces to review this report and systematically examine its implications for their communities and schools. We ask states to consider new mechanisms for providing the incentives that will be required to bring about local collaboration between schools and community agencies.

We urge the President and other national leaders to study the recommendations of this report with a view to establishing a comprehensive federal policy for youth development, including funds for research and demonstration projects; support for pre- and in-service teacher education; full funding for successful existing programs serving middle grade students, such as the Chapter I program for disadvantaged youth; and, along with states and local school districts, relief from compliance with nonessential regulations that inhibit experimentation within individual schools willing to test the ideas contained in this report.

We call upon the private and philanthropic sectors, including foundations, to continue to support new ideas and expand their efforts in the implementation of policies designed to render early adolescence a fruitful period for every young person. The Task Force recommends the establishment of a national forum, with regional equivalents, to monitor the development of new approaches and share information with those interested in transforming middle grade schools. We also recommend the creation of trusts, supported through private and public funds, to support experiments in middle grade innovations in states and communities.

We call upon parents to become involved in defining goals, monitoring their children's studies, and evaluating the progress of the entire school. We urge parents to bring pressure for change in education, health care, and school-community partnerships. We urge parents, and other tax-payers, to support public schools and to demand from schools far better performance than schools now deliver.

Finally, we call upon all those deeply concerned about young adolescents' future, and the future of this nation, to begin now to create the nationwide constituency required to give American young adolescents the preparation they need for life in the 21st century.

The work of all these sectors will be necessary to transform middle grade schools. Through their efforts, a community of learning can be created that engages those young adolescents for whom life already holds high promise, and welcomes into the mainstream of society those who might otherwise be left behind.

THE WORLD IS BEING RAPIDLY transformed by science and technology in ways that have profound significance for our economic well-being and for a democratic society. One upshot is that work will require much technical competence and a great deal of flexibility; not just one set of skills acquired early and essentially good for life, but adaptability to an evolving body of knowledge and new opportunities calling for greatly modified skills. Successful participation in a technically based and interdependent world economy will require that we have a more skillful and adaptable workforce than ever before — at every level from the factory floor to top management.

In the years immediately ahead, the national cohort of young people will be smaller than in recent decades. Fewer college-age students will enter the workforce. By the year 2000, about one-third of these young people will be Black or Hispanic, the groups now at the bottom of the educational and economic ladder. We need to develop the talent of *all* our people if this nation is to be economically competitive and socially cohesive in the different world of the next century.

To do so, we must take advantage of the neglected opportunity provided by the fascinating period of early adolescence, ages 10 to 15 years. This is a time not only of inordinate vulnerability, but also of great responsiveness to environmental challenge. So it provides an exceptional chance for constructive interventions that can have lifelong influence.

The onset of adolescence is a critical period of biological and psychological change for the individual. Puberty is one of the most far-reaching biological upheavals in the life span. For many young adolescents, it involves drastic changes in the social environment as well, foremost among them the transition from elementary to secondary school. These years are highly formative for behavior patterns in education and health that have enduring significance. Adolescence is typically characterized by exploratory behavior, much of which is developmentally appropriate and socially adaptive for most young people. However, many of these behaviors carry high risks. The adverse effects may be near-term and vivid, such as school dropout or alcohol-related accidents. Or they may be long-term, such as bad health habits that lead to heart disease and cancer.

There is a crucial need to help adolescents at this early age to acquire durable self-esteem, flexible and inquiring habits of mind, reliable and relatively close human relationships, a sense of belonging in a valued group, and a sense of usefulness in some way beyond the self. They need to find constructive expression of their inherent curiosity and exploratory energy; and they need a basis for making informed, deliberate decisions — especially on matters that have large consequences, such as educational futures and drug use.

The challenge for educational and related institutions is thus to help provide the building blocks of adolescent development and preparation for adult life. Yet most American junior high and middle schools do not meet the developmental needs of young adolescents. These institutions have the potential to make a tremendous impact on the development of their students — for better or for worse — yet they have been largely ignored in the recent surge of educational reform. As currently organized, these middle grades constitute an arena of casualties — damaging to both students and teachers. Recent research notes a range of negative indicators — all of which have alarming implications for students' engagement and satisfaction with education — around the time that most children move from elementary to either a junior high or middle school.

Most young adolescents attend massive, impersonal schools, learn from unconnected and seemingly irrelevant curricula, know well and trust few adults in school, and lack access to health care and counseling. Millions of these young people fail to receive the guidance and attention they need to become healthy, thoughtful, and productive adults.

We have tolerated this situation for many years, but now our society is changing dramatically. Young adolescents are far more at risk for self-destructive behaviors — educational failure, drug and alcohol abuse, school age pregnancy, contraction of sexually transmitted diseases, violence — than their age group ever was before. Our schools are simply not producing young adolescents who have learned to adopt healthy lifestyles. Moreover, our schools are producing all too few young adolescents with higher skill levels and problem-solving abilities that the economy increasingly needs. The time has come for a fundamental reassessment of this pivotal institution in the lives of these young people.

TASK FORCE REPORT FILLS A GAP

CARNEGIE CORPORATION OF NEW York established the Carnegie Council on Adolescent Development in 1986 to place the compelling challenges of the adolescent years higher on the nation's agenda. In 1987, as its first major commitment, the Council established the Task Force on Education of Young Adolescents under the chairmanship of David W. Hornbeck, former Maryland Superintendent of Schools and a nationally recognized leader in education. Members were drawn from education, research, government, health, and the nonprofit and philanthropic sectors. The Task Force commissioned papers, interviewed experts in relevant fields, and met with teachers, principals, health professionals, and leaders of youth-serving community organizations. It examined, first-hand, promising new approaches to fostering the education and healthy development of young adolescents.

The result is a ground-breaking report that fills a serious gap in reports on education reform in the 1980s. The report reinforces an emerging movement, still relatively unrecognized by policymakers, to build support for and educate young adolescents through new relationships between schools, families, and health and community institutions.

The recommendations in this report engage people at all levels of society in this movement: the President and the Congress; officials of state and local governments; members of boards of education, superintendents, administrators, principals, and teachers; health professionals and leaders of youth-serving and community organizations; and parents and students themselves. The report indicates ways in which these groups can help accomplish a fundamental upgrading of education and adolescent development.

The emerging adolescent is caught in turbulence, a fascinated but perplexed observer of the biological, psychological, and social changes swirling all around. In groping for a solid path toward a worthwhile adult life, adolescents can grasp the middle grade school as the crucial and reliable handle. Now, the middle grade school must change, and change substantially, to cope with the requirements of a new era — to give its students a decent chance in life and to help them fulfill their youthful promise. This is a daunting task but a feasible one. This report will be a great help to those who wish to make this goal a practical reality.

David A. Hamburg
President, Carnegie Corporation of New York
Chair, Carnegie Council on Adolescent Development
New York
June 1989

THIS REPORT EXAMINES THE condition of America's young adolescents and how well middle grade schools, health institutions, and community organizations serve them. The Task Force makes recommendations for new structures for middle grade education, which the Task Force believes will help to preserve a strong and vital America.

Before proceeding, however, it is useful to consider our goal. What qualities do we envision in the 15-year-old who has been well served in the middle years of schooling? What do we want every young adolescent to know, to feel, to be able to do upon emerging from that educational and school-related experience?

Our answer is embodied in five characteristics associated with being an effective human being. Our 15-year-old will be:

▲ An intellectually reflective person;
▲ A person enroute to a lifetime of meaningful work;
▲ A good citizen;
▲ A caring and ethical individual; and
▲ A healthy person.

THE YOUNG ADOLESCENT IS maturing intellectually at a significant rate. Our youth will be able to analyze problems and issues, examine the component parts, and reintegrate them into either a solution or into a new way of stating the problem or issue. In developing thinking skills, the youth will master self-expression and be able to "hear" others' expressions through diverse media. These skills of self-expression and hearing include persuasive and coherent writing, articulate verbal expression, and familiarity with symbols and basic vocabularies of the arts, mathematics, and the sciences. Moreover, the student will be able to appreciate and absorb the perspectives of cultures (and languages) different from his or her own.

OUR YOUNG ADOLESCENT WILL begin to understand work as both the means of economic survival and an important source of one's identity. The youth will be increasingly aware of career and occupation options, not feeling bound by restrictions of race, gender, or ethnicity. Each will understand that high school graduation is a prerequisite to being competitive in the adult workforce and will begin to understand the advantages of postsecondary education. Perhaps most importantly, the youth will have learned to learn, a critically important capacity because of the rapidly changing nature of occupations and jobs. Finally, the youth will have pursued a course of study and developed cognitively in a manner that maintains all career options.

OUR YOUNG ADOLESCENT WILL BE a good citizen in three ways. First, our 15-year-old will accept responsibility for shaping and not simply being shaped by surrounding events. Central to demonstrating good citizenship is a youth who is a doer, not just an observer. The youth will, for example, demonstrate good citizenship by helping to determine the nature and character of his or her own school community.

A second reflection of the young adolescent's good citizenship will be an understanding of the genesis and history of the United States and its basic values, such as the principles of democracy upon which the nation is built. In understanding these values, the youth will be able to assess the degree to which the nation practiced those values historically and practices them today. The youth will understand the way government in the United States functions at the local, state, and federal levels and will participate in appropriate ways in creating and maintaining a healthy community.

Finally, our young adolescent's good citizenship will be embodied in a positive sense of global citizenship. That involvement will reflect an appreciation of both the Western and non-Western worlds. The youth will possess a feeling of personal responsibility for and connection to the well-being of an interdependent world community.

OUR 15-YEAR-OLD WILL NOT ONLY have developed the capacity to think clearly and critically, but will also have learned to act ethically. The youth will recognize that there is good and bad and that it is possible and important to tell the difference. The youth will exhibit the courage to discern the difference as a normal part of daily life and to act on the conclusions reached.

The young person will embrace many virtues such as courage, acceptance of responsibility, honesty, integrity, tolerance, appreciation of individual differences, and caring about others. The young person will demonstrate all these values through sustained service to others.

Finally, our 15-year-old will understand the importance of developing and maintaining close relationships with certain other people, including friends and family, relationships of the character that require great effort and even sacrifice, but without which life is filled with insecurity and loneliness.

THE 15-YEAR-OLD WE ENVISION will be physically and mentally fit. Exercise, diet, and proper health consultation and care will nurture a youth whose physical and mental health needs have been understood and met. Equally important, our young adolescent will have a self-image of competence and strength. This self-image will be based on the fact that the youth will be at least very good at something, because success is critical to a positive self-image. The youth's field of success may be academic or extracurricular, vocational or avocational, community or familial.

In addition, our young person will have developed self-understanding, rejoicing in the knowledge of personal strengths and enroute to overcoming weaknesses. A combination of self-understanding and a positive self-image, taken with other skills in the individual's repertoire, will equip the youth with appropriate coping skills.

We have described the young adolescent we envision. Our vision is of such an outcome for *every* youth of the nation, not just for those more advantaged than others. Every human being has the capacity to achieve significant success, not just minimum competence, in each of the five areas.

Our 15-year-old is a thinking, productive, caring, and healthy person who takes seriously the responsibility of good citizenship. The challenge of the 1990s is to define and create the structures of teaching and learning for young adolescents 10 to 15 years old that will yield mature young people of competence, compassion, and promise.

David W. Hornbeck
Chair, Task Force on Education of Young Adolescents
Baltimore
June 1989

FATEFUL CHOICES FOR YOUNG ADOLESCENTS AND THE NATION

Young adolescents today make fateful choices, fateful for them and for our nation. The period of life from ages 10 to 15 represents for many young people their last best chance to choose a path toward productive and fulfilling lives.

Depending on family circumstances, household income, language, neighborhood, or the color of their skin, some of these young adolescents receive the education and support they need to develop self-respect, an active mind, and a healthy body. They will emerge from their teens as the promising youth who will become the scientists and entrepreneurs, the educators and health care professionals, and the parents who will renew the nation. These are the thoughtful, responsible, caring, ethical, and robust young people the Task Force envisions. To them, society can entrust the future of the country with confidence.

Under current conditions, however, far too many young people will not make the passage through early adolescence successfully. Their basic human needs — caring relationships with adults, guidance in facing sometimes overwhelming biological and psychological changes, the security of belonging to constructive peer groups, and the perception of future opportunity — go unmet at this critical stage of life. Millions of these young adolescents will never reach their full potential.

Early adolescence for these youth is a turning point towards a diminished future. Many will live outside or on the fringes of those communities that produce the achievers and the leaders in this society. A substantial number will grow into adults who are alienated from other people, who have low expectations for themselves and for whom society has low expectations, and who are likely to produce in uncommon share the unhealthy, the addicted, the criminal, the violent, and the chronically poor. These are the youth left behind.

In even the most affluent communities, young adolescents display the attitudes and behavior that portend difficulty. Such young people often drop out of school or participate at such a low level of effort that, even if they graduate, they have few marketable skills. They may abuse alcohol or drugs, or engage in other antisocial or criminal conduct. For many of us who ought to be concerned, however, daily life is too demanding, change comes too rapidly, money is too plentiful for us to care about troubled teenagers, school dropouts, juvenile offenders, or adolescents who can neither read nor write nor choose to participate fully in school.

Apart from our moral responsibility, we also face an economic imperative to ensure that these young people are properly educated. With the numbers of elderly rising rapidly, the economy cannot support both swelling ranks of the retired and endless additions to the unemployed and the underemployed. Response to drug addiction, crime, violence, and teenage pregnancy continues to consume substantial national resources. With the need for literate and skilled workers increasing, and the pool of such people decreasing, business and industry cannot idly watch a new generation of potential workers slide into chronically unproductive lives.

Who are these young people left behind? How do they differ from their counterparts who enter the later teen years so ready for the demands of life? Why are some youth so well and others so ill prepared for their future? Answers to these questions begin with an understanding of what it means to be a young adolescent in America as the 21st century approaches.

BY AGE 15, MILLIONS OF AMERICAN youth are at risk of reaching adulthood unable to meet adequately the requirements of the workplace, the commitments of relationships in families and with peers, and the responsibilities of participation in a multicultural society and of citizenship in a democracy. These young people often suffer from underdeveloped intellectual abilities, indifference to good health, and cynicism about the values that American society embodies.

These characteristics of a critical mass of young people in this country are apparent to any observer. What is less clear, because this period has until recently been the least understood of any stage of life, are the causes of this alienation.

During early adolescence, many youth enter a period of trial and error, of vulnerability to emotional hurt and humiliation, of anxiety and uncertainty that are sources of unevenness of emotions and behavior associated with the age. Yet the turmoil can herald the emergence of a new individual with the potential to learn, to think critically and independently, and to act responsibly according to principles and a code of ethics.

This time is of immense importance in the development of the young person. Biologically, young adolescents experience puberty, a period of growth and development more rapid than in any other phase of life except infancy. Over four or five years, dramatic changes occur in height, weight, and body composition, and young people acquire the capacity to reproduce. Youth enter puberty at a significantly younger age today than in previous generations. In the United States 150 years ago, the average age of a girl's first menstrual period was 16 years; today it is 12.5 years. The change for boys is less pronounced but follows a similar trend. While they become biologically mature at earlier ages, many young adolescents remain intellectually and emotionally immature. Thus, young people 10, 11, and 12 years old are able to, and do, make fateful choices involving their own sexuality that can affect their entire life course.

YOUNG ADOLESCENTS INCREASINGLY look outward from the home to gain an understanding of themselves and their circumstances. It is here, as they come face-to-face with realities of life in America: The terms and conditions of early adolescence have changed dramatically.

These young people enter a world in which they will likely be tempted, if not pressured, to experiment with drugs and alcohol. They may live in neighborhoods so dangerous that they fear walking to school. They date earlier in life than their parents did. They are at once admonished to control their sexual urges and bombarded through the media with the allure of sex. They are challenged to make the ideals and values of a just society their own, yet made painfully aware that money and power are the keys to success. They begin to assess their prospects and to decide how much to invest in their future by staying in school and keeping out of trouble. They begin to perceive their own future either as promising or as hard, bleak, and empty of opportunity.

In our changed America, the sense of community that once existed in urban neighborhoods and in some rural towns has eroded. Stable, close-knit communities where people know and look out for each other are far less common than they were a generation or two ago. Although the economy continues to expand and jobs are plentiful, the unskilled can find only low-paying work. Many families struggle to maintain their standard of living and often sacrifice time with each other. Family structures have changed dramatically, as both divorce and single-parent households are far more common than a decade ago. Families and individuals move frequently to find jobs, affordable housing, or other opportunities. The workplace has changed, as more women work outside the home and people switch jobs more often. Whole industries have disappeared in recent years.

In these times of rapid change, when young people face unprecedented choices and pressures, adult guidance is all too often withdrawn. Many parents, seeing that their child is developing in profound ways, mistake the stirring of independent thinking for the capacity to make adult decisions. They do not realize that their child's needs for autonomy require not rejection of filial bonds, but a realignment of roles and relationships within the family.

The young adolescent is moving from dependency to interdependency with parents, as well as with friends, relatives, and other persons outside the home. While renegotiating relationships with parents and other care-givers, often in outwardly stormy ways, the young person simultaneously seeks to maintain strong ties with exactly those people.

Freed from the dependency of childhood, but not yet able to find their own path to adulthood, many young people feel a desperate sense of isolation. Surrounded only by their equally confused peers, too many make poor decisions with harmful or lethal consequences.

YOUNG ADOLESCENTS TODAY FACE GREATER RISKS

DURING EARLY ADOLESCENCE, ALL youth are caught in a vortex of new risks. They face risks that were almost unknown to their parents or grandparents, and face those risks at an early age. Many youth today first experiment with tobacco, alcohol, and illicit drugs during early adolescence. For example, 92 percent of the high school class of 1987 had begun drinking before graduating; of those, 56 percent had begun drinking in the 6th to 9th grades and 36 percent in the 10th to 12th grades.[1] (See Figure 1.) These data do not include those youth who dropped out before graduating high school, a population even more

UNTITLED

By Jeremy Patrick Murphy

The tears are useless, I know;
    But somewhere, far back
    In my mind, I cry anyway.

There is a feeling, horribly absolute,
    Of unchangeable impotence.
    There is love, yes. . . .

One half of it, at least.
    But the air is silent;
    Where is the other call of the horn?

I do not know, and I almost cease to care;
    My life is melancholy, terribly alone
    — I need someone.

But wait! I am wrong:
    I do not cease to care,
    But rather transfer that care to a deeper, more
        intimate place.

Somewhere far back in my mind,
    The unfathomable depths,
    There is a glimmer of faint hope.

Then it is gone, and again the other comes:
    The wave of blackness,
    Leaving me awash in despair.

My life is a balance, an equilibrium:
    But one gone mad.
    That chaotic dissonance prevails.

I feel as if it is a scale,
    Tipped violently by God,
    Swinging back and forth:

Or a pendulum that knows no bounds,
    Governing my life with its mountains and valleys;
    It is orderly anarchy that rules.

I wonder sometimes,
    If I judge myself too harshly:
    What answer is there ever, what honest response?

I also wonder many times,
    If I am hypocritical,
    If I should perhaps leap from a bridge somewhere over
        some nameless river. . . .

Is there an answer anywhere?
    None to be found, it seems:
    I am in a quandary:

A dilemma which I cannot escape.
    There is always a cloud on the horizon,
    Or a patch of blue;

But now I am lost,
    For I cannot even see the horizon.
    Would that I had eyes that saw!

I am blinded by that basest of emotions,
    My nose turned toward a dark alley by some hand of
        Fate,
    I step blindly, timidly, uncertainly forward.

At the end of that alley,
    I may find a rainbow and a pot of gold:
    Or, as the darkness disappears, perhaps just another
        busy highway.

I don't know.

Grade 8, Oakland Junior High School
Columbia, Missouri
Patricia Beeson, Teacher

Figure 1. 1987 High School Graduates: Grade of First Use for Cigarettes, Alcohol and Illicit Drugs

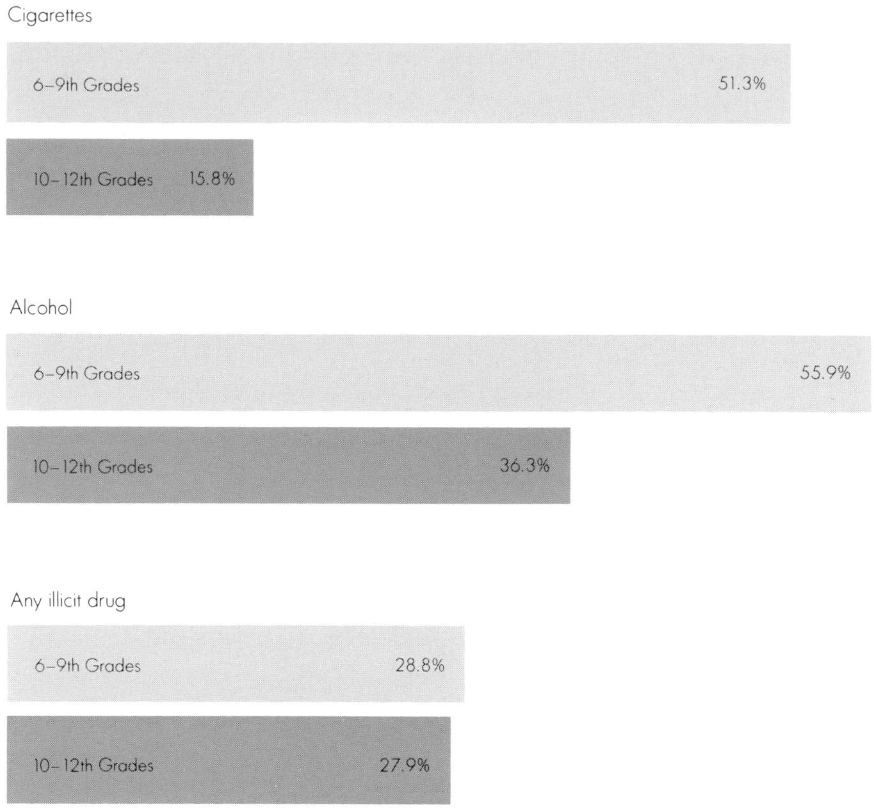

Cigarettes

6–9th Grades — 51.3%

10–12th Grades — 15.8%

Alcohol

6–9th Grades — 55.9%

10–12th Grades — 36.3%

Any illicit drug

6–9th Grades — 28.8%

10–12th Grades — 27.9%

Johnston, L. D., O'Malley, P. M., & Bachman, J. G. (1988). *Illicit drug use, smoking and drinking by America's high school students, college students, and young adults: 1975–1987* (DHHS Publication No. (ADM) 89–1602). Washington, DC: U.S. Government Printing Office.

Figure 2. Proportion of 1944–1946 and 1962–1964 Female Birth Cohorts Initiating Sexual Activity at Specific Ages, By Race

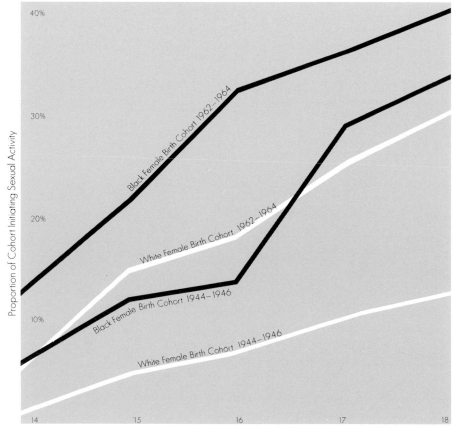

Hofferth, S. L., Kahn, J. R., & Baldwin, W. (1987). Premarital sexual activity among U.S. teenage women over the past three decades. *Family Planning Perspectives, 19*(2), 46–53.

prone to early use of alcohol and drugs. In the short term, drug use may interfere with physical development, motivation, and ability to concentrate in school, and may impair judgment about risky behaviors. The fact that so many youth are involved with drugs and alcohol at such young ages is alarming because of compelling evidence that drug use in early adolescence is a critical factor in long-term substance abuse.[2]

More and more teenagers below the age of 16 are becoming sexually active.[3] (See Figure 2.) Partners face extremely high risks of the young woman becoming pregnant. These pregnancies lead disproportionately to the birth of low-weight babies who are vulnerable to a variety of poor outcomes. Moreover, these young mothers tend to drop out of school early. This fact, along with economic disadvantage, often limits future opportunities for many of these women.[4]

Besides the risk of pregnancy, young people are in serious jeopardy of contracting sexually transmitted diseases. Fully one-fourth of all sexually active adolescents will become infected with a sexually transmitted disease before graduating from high school, a grave situation that makes AIDS a potential timebomb for millions of American youth.[5]

Motor vehicle and other accidents, taken together, are the leading causes of death among young people 10 to 14 years of age.[6] (See Figure 3.) Substance abuse and risk-taking behavior account for many of these accidents, as does association with older adolescents involved in such behavior, especially while driving. Between 1980 and 1985, the suicide rate more than doubled for 10- to 14-year-olds, although suicide remains one of the least likely causes of death for early adolescents.[7] Seriously delinquent activities rise during early adolescence and peak at age 15.[8]

Many problem behaviors of young adolescents appear to be interrelated. Young people who smoke and drink often experiment with illegal drugs and early, unprotected sex as well. These same young people are also prone to school failure.[9] They are not merely exploring new behaviors, in short, but trying out lifestyles that become more entrenched as they grow older.[10]

ALTHOUGH ALL YOUNG PEOPLE FACE significant stress in early adolescence, many reach late adolescence relatively unscathed.[11] But many others fail to develop the intellectual capacities and coping skills that they will need to meet the demands of adult life.

POVERTY AND DISCRIMINATION ADD TO RISK

The risks that all young people face are compounded for those who are poor, members of racial or ethnic minorities, or recent immigrants. These youth generally attend the weakest schools, have access to the least adequate health services, and have the fewest clearly visible paths to opportunities in the mainstream.

Rates of retention in grade (being kept back a year) — a school practice directly related to students' dropping out[12] — are far higher among minority youth in the middle grades. (See Figure 4.) For many of these young people, the decision to drop out is clearly made before they

Figure 3. Causes of Mortality in 10–14 Year Olds: By Race (1985)

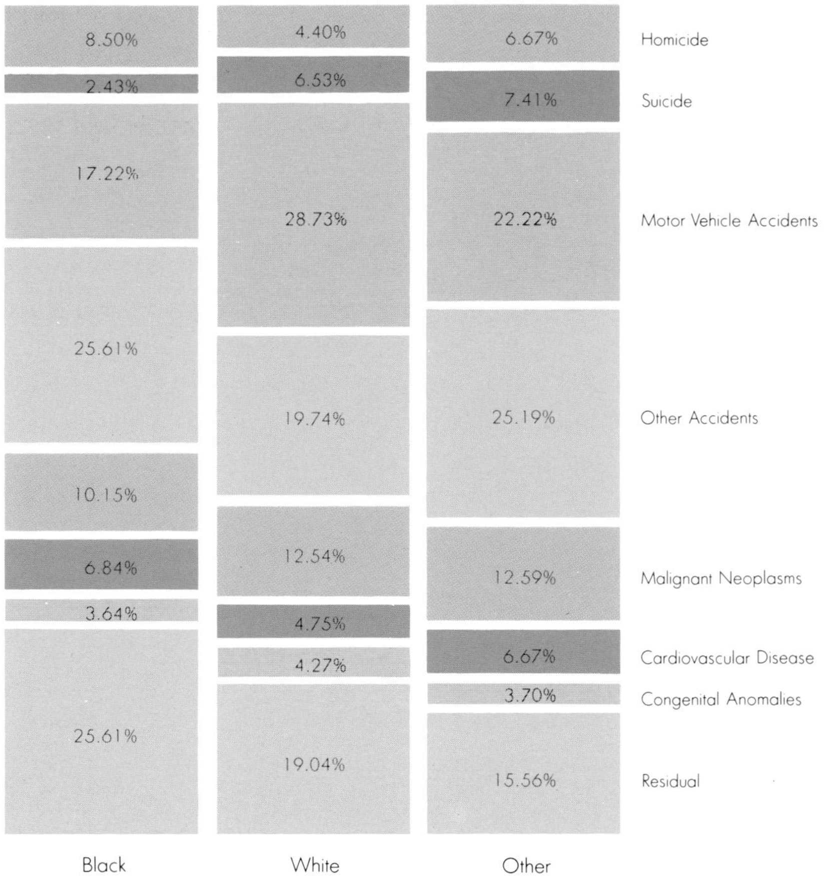

Chartbook on adolescent health. (in press). Rockville, MD: Public Health Service, Health Resources and Services Administration, Bureau of Health Care Delivery and Assistance, Division of Maternal and Child Health.

	Black	White	Other	
Homicide	8.50%	4.40%	6.67%	
Suicide	2.43%	6.53%	7.41%	
Motor Vehicle Accidents	17.22%	28.73%	22.22%	
Other Accidents	25.61%	19.74%	25.19%	
	10.15%			
Malignant Neoplasms	6.84%	12.54%	12.59%	
Cardiovascular Disease	3.64%	4.75%	6.67%	
Congenital Anomalies		4.27%	3.70%	
Residual	25.61%	19.04%	15.56%	

Figure 4. Percentage of 13-Year-Old Students in the U.S. Who Are 1 or More Years Below Expected Grade Level, By Race (October 1986)

U.S. Bureau of the Census. (1988). *School enrollment — social and economic characteristics of students: October 1986.* (Current Population Report, Series P-20, No. 429). Washington, DC: U.S. Government Printing Office.

Female

Hispanic (any race)   41.2%

Black   33.1%

White   22.2%

Male

Hispanic (any race)   46.8%

Black   44.0%

White   29.6%

begin high school. An estimated 59 percent of Hispanic dropouts leave school before completing the 10th grade. [13] (See Figure 5.) Data from one school system, Washington, D.C., which is seeking to understand its dropout problem through careful research, show that more than half of all dropouts leave before completing the 10th grade. Ninety-two percent of all students in the Washington, D.C., school system are Black.[14] (See Figure 6.)

It is not acceptable that minority youth are chronically the worst educated in our society. By the year 2020, because of higher birth rates among minority populations and patterns of immigration, nearly half of all school-aged children will be non-White.[15] Continuing to allow minority youth to face extraordinary risks of failure is a direct threat to our national standard of living and democratic foundations.

NO DEFINITIVE STATISTICS EXIST on the numbers of youth at risk of unhealthy and unproductive lives. Recent first attempts at estimating these numbers indicate, however, that of the 28 million girls and boys ages 10 to 17 in the United States, about 7 million may be extremely vulnerable to the negative consequences of multiple high-risk behaviors such as school failure, substance abuse, and early unprotected intercourse. Thus it is estimated that the future of about 7 million youth — one in four adolescents — is in serious jeopardy.

Another 7 million may be at moderate risk, because of occasional substance use and early but more often protected intercourse. About half of the nation's youth are at low risk of engaging in seriously damaging behaviors. They may, however, require strong and consistent support to avoid becoming involved in these problems.[16]

That half our nation's youth is at serious or moderate risk is cause enough for alarm. But even among those at little or no risk of damaging behaviors, the pervasiveness of intellectual underdevelopment strikes at the heart of our nation's future prosperity. American 13-year-olds, for example, are now on average far behind their counterparts in other industrialized nations in mathematics and science achievement.[17] (See Figures 7 and 8.)

Most distressing is the fact that the critical reasoning skills of many American young adolescents are extremely deficient. A recent National Assessment of Educational Progress (NAEP) found that only 11 percent of 13-year-olds were "adept" readers, that is, able to understand relatively complicated written information.[18] In NAEP tests requiring analytic or persuasive writing, fewer than one in five 8th graders wrote adequate or better essays. The study concluded, ". . . students at all grade levels are deficient in higher order thinking skills."[19]

The economy will increasingly have little use for youth who are impaired by high-risk behaviors or who are intellectually unprepared for the challenges of a changing economy. Job growth is concentrated in occupations that require much more than basic literacy. Three million of the 27 million new jobs created between 1972 and 1986 required only a

Figure 5. Of U.S. Hispanic Dropouts Aged 14–25, Estimated Percentage Completing Grades 5–11 at Time of Departure: Spring 1976*

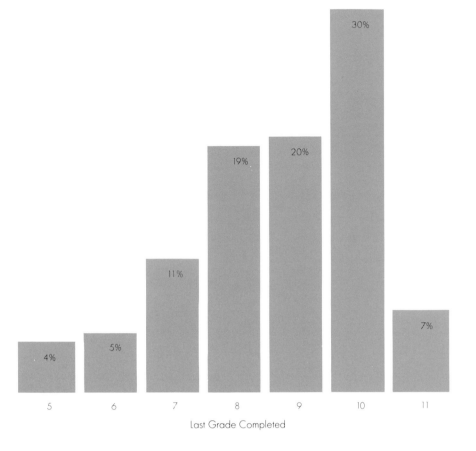

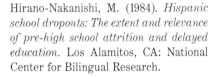

Hirano-Nakanishi, M. (1984). *Hispanic school dropouts: The extent and relevance of pre-high school attrition and delayed education.* Los Alamitos, CA: National Center for Bilingual Research.

*Enrollment data originally reported as grade at time of departure from school. Dropouts' last grade completed was determined as the grade prior to their grade at time of departure.

Figure 6. Of Dropouts from Washington, DC Public Schools, Estimated Percentage Completing Grades 5–11 at Time of Departure

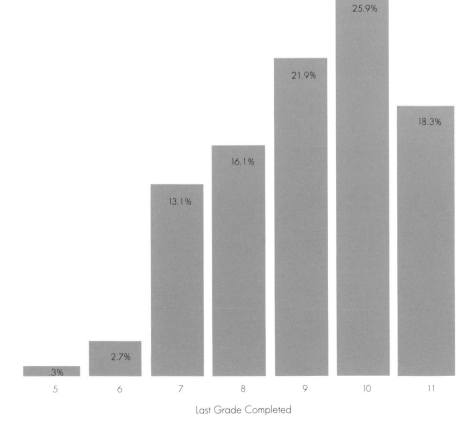

Jenkins, A.E., III. (1988, October). *A study of students who left: D.C. public school dropouts.* Washington, DC: District of Columbia Public Schools, Division of Quality Assurance and Management Planning.

basic level of literacy. More than 10 million of the new jobs were in professional, technical, administrative and managerial occupations, and the remaining 14 million were in sales, clerical, and crafts.[20]

The domestic job market today reflects the intense international competition in which the United States finds itself. This nation needs a workforce capable of critical thinking and creative problem-solving. Yet we continue to educate youth for the smokestack economy of generations past.

As a nation, therefore, we face a paradox of our own making. We have created an economy that seeks literate, technically trained, and committed workers, while simultaneously we produce many young men and women who are semi-literate or functionally illiterate, unable to think critically and untrained in technical skills, hampered by high-risk lifestyles, and alienated from the social mainstream. Unemployment rates for high school dropouts are more than twice those for high school graduates.[21] The few jobs for which these people qualify often pay too little to support a family.* For many of these young people, the American dream ends with the recognition that they are not wanted and are of little value in this society.

What is left for these young men and women is a life on the edge of society. Those with minimal competencies will barely get by. The most poorly prepared will move in and out of crime, drug abuse, or alcoholism. Some will be forced to depend on government assistance in one form or another — income maintenance, health care, and housing. Many will pay little in taxes and will be able to contribute little to Social Security or to caring for themselves in their later years.

*In 1986, fewer than half (44 percent) of all young men ages 20 to 24 earned enough to support a family of 3 above the poverty line, down from 58 percent in 1973. Fewer than one-quarter (24 percent) of all Black men ages 20 to 24 had earnings above the 3-person poverty line, down from 54 percent in 1973.[22]

COSTS OF PREVENTABLE PROBLEMS

School Dropout

▲ Each year's class of dropouts will, over their lifetime, cost the nation about $260 billion in lost earnings and foregone taxes.[23]

▲ In a lifetime, a male high school dropout will earn $260,000 less than a high school graduate, and contribute $78,000 less in taxes. A female who does not finish high school will earn $200,000 less, and contribute $60,000 less in taxes.[24]

▲ Unemployment rates for high school dropouts are more than twice those of high school graduates. Between 1973 and 1986, young people who did not finish

high school suffered a 42 percent drop in annual earnings in constant 1986 dollars.[25]

▲ Each added year of secondary education reduces the probability of public welfare dependency in adulthood by 35 percent.[26]

Teenage Pregnancy

▲ The United States spent more than $19 billion in 1987 in payments for income maintenance, health care, and nutrition to support families begun by teenagers.[27]

▲ Babies born to teen mothers are at heightened risk of low birthweight. Initial hospital care

for low-birthweight infants averages $20,000. Total lifetime medical costs for low-birthweight infants averages $400,000.[28]

▲ Of teens who give birth, 46 percent will go on welfare within four years; of unmarried teens who give birth, 73 percent will be on welfare within four years.[29]

Alcohol and Drug Abuse

▲ Alcohol and drug abuse in the United States cost more than $136 billion in 1980 in reduced productivity, treatment, crime, and related costs.[30]

Figure 7. Average Science Proficiency of 13-Year-Olds in 5 Countries and 4 Canadian Provinces

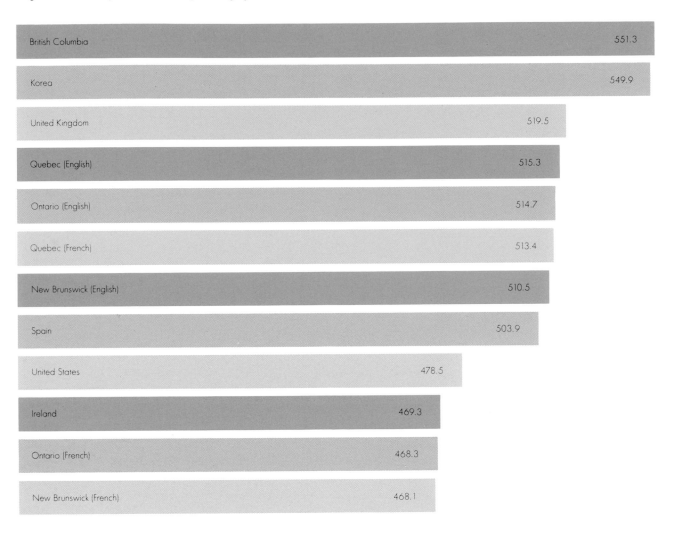

Lapointe, A. E., Mead, N. A., & Phillips, G. W. (1989, January). *A world of differences: An international assessment of mathematics and science.* Princeton, NJ: Educational Testing Service.

Students' science proficiency was determined on the basis of their response to 60 questions drawn from the 1986 National Assessment of Educational Progress. Overall performance is summarized as an average proficiency score for each of the 12 populations assessed, expressed on a hypothetical scale ranging from 0 to 1,000 (mean = 500, s.d. = 100). For purposes of interpretation, five "anchor" points are defined:

Level 300

Know Everyday Science Facts — Students, for example, exhibit rudimentary knowledge concerning the environment and animals.

Level 400

Understand and Apply Simple Scientific Principles — Students exhibit a growing knowledge in the Life Sciences; can apply some basic principles from the Physical Sciences.

Level 500

Use Scientific Procedures and Analyze Scientific Data — Students understand the use of experimental procedures and can identify the best conclusions based on observed phenomena.

Level 600

Understand and Apply Intermediate Scientific Knowledge and Principles — Students can apply understanding of scientific principles to design experiments and interpret data. They can also interpret figures used to convey scientific information.

Level 700

Integrate Scientific Information and Experimental Evidence — Students can interpret experimental data that involves several variables. They also can interrelate data represented in a variety of forms — text, graphs, figures and diagrams.

Figure 8. Average Mathematics Proficiency of 13-Year-Olds in 5 Countries and 4 Canadian Provinces

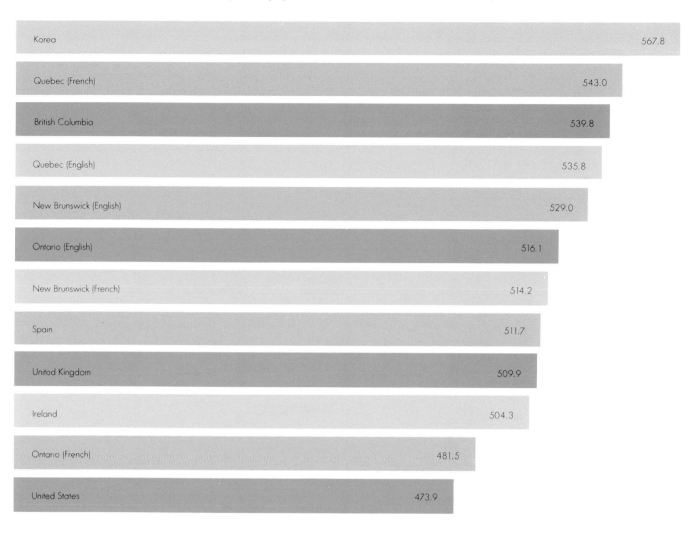

Lapointe, A. E., Mead, N. A., & Phillips, G. W. (1989, January). *A world of differences: An international assessment of mathematics and science.* Princeton, NJ: Educational Testing Service.

Students' mathematics proficiency was determined on the basis of their response to 63 questions drawn from the 1986 National Assessment of Educational Progress. Overall performance is summarized as an average proficiency score for each of the 12 populations assessed expressed on a hypothetical scale ranging from 0 to 1,000 (mean = 500, s.d. = S100). For purposes of interpretation, five "anchor" points are defined.

Level 300
Perform Simple Addition and Subtraction — Students can add and subtract two-digit numbers and solve simple number sentences involving these operations.

Level 400
Use Basic Operations to Solve Problems — Students can select appropriate basic operations to solve simple one-step problems. They can understand the most basic concepts of logic, estimation and geometry.

Level 500
Use Intermediate Mathematics Skills to Solve Two-Step Problems—Students demonstrate an understanding of the concept of order, place, value; they know some properties of odd and even numbers and of zero; and they can apply elementary concepts of ration and proportion.

Level 600
Understand Measurement and Geometry Concepts and Solve More Complex Problems — Students know how to multiply fractions and decimals and are able to use a range of procedures to solve more complex problems.

Level 700
Understand and Apply More Advanced Mathematical Concepts — Students can deal with proportion of the arithmetic mean and can use data from a complex table to solve problems. They demonstrate an increasing ability to apply school-based skills to out-of-school situations and problems.

The specter of a divided society—one affluent, the other poor—looms ominously on the American horizon. Inherent in this scenario is the potential for serious conflict between generations, among races and ethnic groups, and between the economically disfranchised and middle- and upper-income groups. It is a disturbing scenario that must not occur.

MIDDLE GRADE SCHOOLS HAVE BEEN virtually ignored in discussions of educational reform in the past decade. Yet, they are central not only to channeling every young adolescent into the mainstream of life in American communities, but also to making vast improvements in academic and personal outcomes for all youth.

Middle grade schools—junior high, intermediate, or middle schools—are potentially society's most powerful force to recapture millions of youth adrift. Yet all too often they exacerbate the problems youth face.

A volatile mismatch exists between the organization and curriculum of middle grade schools, and the intellectual, emotional, and interpersonal needs of young adolescents.[31] For most young adolescents, the shift from elementary to junior high or middle school means moving from a small, neighborhood school and the stability of one primary classroom to a much larger, more impersonal institution, typically at a greater distance from home. In this new setting, teachers and classmates will change as many as six or seven times a day. This constant shifting creates formidable barriers to the formation of stable peer groups and close, supportive relationships with caring adults.[32] The chances that young people will feel lost are enormous. Today, as young adolescents move from elementary to middle or junior high schools, their involvement with learning diminishes and their rates of alienation, drug abuse, absenteeism, and dropping out begin to rise. The warning signals are there to see.

The ability of young adolescents to cope is often further jeopardized by a middle grade curriculum that assumes a need for an intellectual moratorium during early adolescence. Some educators consider the young adolescent incapable of critical, complex thought during rapid physical and emotional development. Minimal effort, they argue, should be spent to stimulate higher levels of thought and decisionmaking until the youth reaches high school and becomes teachable again. Existing knowledge seriously challenges these assumptions.[33] Yet many middle grade schools fail to recognize or to act on this knowledge.

Furthermore, many middle grade schools pay little attention to the emotional, physical, and social development of their students. Young adolescents need proper nutrition, health, and social services to maintain good physical and mental health and fitness. Students who are hungry, sick, troubled, or depressed cannot function well in the classroom, no matter how good the school. Moreover, young adolescents need adult guidance to help them cope with one of life's more confusing periods.

Middle grade schools cannot meet all these needs alone. To fulfill their vital functions, they will need to operate at the center of a network of community resources that includes local government, health services, youth-serving organizations, private businesses, and the philanthropic sector. In many localities today, that network does not exist, and middle grade schools are unable to meet their responsibilities to their students or to the community.

Caring is crucial to the development of young adolescents into healthy adults. Young adolescents need to see themselves as valued members of a group that offers mutual support and trusting relationships. They need to be able to succeed at something, and to be praised and rewarded for that success. They need to become socially competent individuals who have the skills to cope successfully with the exigencies of everyday life. They need to believe that they have a promising future, and they need the competence to take advantage of real opportunities in a society in which they have a stake.

This report examines and begins to develop responses to the distinctive needs of young adolescents in America today. It sets out recommendations for a fundamental transformation in middle grade schools and in relations among parents, schools, and communities that could benefit every student. This transformation is intended to create for every young person a community that engages those for whom life already holds high promise, and welcomes into the mainstream of society those who might otherwise be left behind.

TRANSFORMING THE EDUCATION OF YOUNG ADOLESCENTS

Many middle grade schools today fall far short of meeting the critical educational, health, and social needs of millions of young adolescents. Many youth now leave the middle grades unprepared for what lies ahead of them. A fundamental transformation of the education of young adolescents is urgently required.

Young adolescents have a great need for intimacy, yet we put them in large, impersonal schools. Young adolescents need increased autonomy and they need to make their own decisions, yet we put them in environments of review and rote learning. Young adolescents show great variability among themselves and within themselves, yet we put them in classrooms where we ignore their variability and need for flexibility.

In reaching its vision of transformed middle grade schools, the Task Force visited or examined sites of middle grades innovation, and met with talented and committed individuals throughout the country who are deeply engaged in making middle grade schools work for young adolescents. Integrating the most current research knowledge with considered and wise practice, the Task Force found that the transformation of education for young adolescents involves eight essential principles:

▲ Large middle grade schools are divided into smaller communities for learning.

▲ Middle grade schools transmit a core of common knowledge to all students.

▲ Middle grade schools are organized to ensure success for all students.

▲ Teachers and principals have the major responsibility and power to transform middle grade schools.

▲ Teachers for the middle grades are specifically prepared to teach young adolescents.

▲ Schools promote good health; the education and health of young adolescents are inextricably linked.

▲ Families are allied with school staff through mutual respect, trust, and communication.

▲ Schools and communities are partners in educating young adolescents.

The middle grade school proposed here is profoundly different from many schools today. It focuses squarely on the characteristics and needs of young adolescents. It creates a community of adults and young people embedded in networks of support and responsibility that enhance the commitment of students to learning. In partnership with youth-serving and community organizations, it offers multiple sites and multiple methods for fostering the learning and health of adolescents. The combined efforts create a community of shared purpose among those concerned that all young adolescents are prepared for productive adult lives, especially those at risk of being left behind.

School should be a place where close, trusting relationships with adults and peers create a climate for personal growth and intellectual development.

MANY LARGE MIDDLE GRADE schools function as mills that contain and process endless streams of students. Within them are masses of anonymous youth. Student populations in a middle grade school exceed 1,000 in many jurisdictions and reach as high as 2,000 in some urban areas.

Such settings virtually guarantee that the intellectual and emotional needs of youth will go unmet. Consider what is asked of these students: Every 50 minutes, perhaps 6 or 7 times each day, assemble with 30 or so of your peers, each time in a different group, sit silently in a chair in neat, frozen rows, and try to catch hold of knowledge as it whizzes by you in the words of an adult you met only at the beginning of this school year. The subject of one class has nothing to do with the subject of the next class. If a concept is confusing, don't ask for help, there isn't time to explain. If something interests you deeply, don't stop to think about it, there's too much to cover. If your feelings of awkwardness about your rapid growth make it difficult to concentrate, keep your concerns to yourself. And don't dare help or even talk to your fellow students in class; that may be considered cheating.

Understandably, teachers are reluctant to offer to work under these conditions, although many are required to do so. Many youth manage to cope and some even flourish within such structures. But many others fall behind.

Three qualities should be infused into such a setting. First, the enormous middle grade school must be restructured in a more human scale. The student should, upon entering middle grade school, join a small community in which people—students and adults—get to know each other well to create a climate for intellectual development. Students should feel that they are part of a community of shared educational purpose.

Second, the discontinuity in expectations and practices among teachers, the lack of integration of subject matter, and the instability of peer groups must be reduced. Every student must be able to rely on a small, caring group of adults who work closely with each other to provide coordinated, meaningful, and challenging educational experiences. In turn, teachers must have the opportunity to get to know every one of their students well enough to understand and teach them as individuals. Every student must have the opportunity to know a variety of peers, some of them well.

Finally, every student needs at least one thoughtful adult who has the time and takes the trouble to talk with the student about academic matters, personal problems, and the importance of performing well in middle grade school. The student who feels overwhelmed by course work, worried about a health problem, intimidated by classmates, or accused of misbehaving needs to be able to confide in someone with experience and access to authority. So does the student who has just scored well on a test, painted a terrific portrait, or earned a berth on an athletic or scholastic team.

The Task Force recommends that middle grade schools develop these qualities by:

▲ Creating smaller learning environments;

▲ Forming teachers and students into teams; and

▲ Assigning an adult advisor to each student.

CREATING SMALLER LEARNING ENVIRONMENTS

ONE SUCCESSFUL SOLUTION TO unacceptably large middle grade schools is the school-within-school or house arrangement. Clearly named and marked areas within the larger building are designated for students and teachers assigned to a particular house.

A house should contain 200 to 300 students but no more than 500. Students in the house would constitute a microcosm of the school population in ethnic and socioeconomic background and in physical, emotional, and intellectual maturity, allowing students to learn from each other about human diversity. Students should remain in the same house as long as they are enrolled in the school, and view themselves as graduates of the house as well as of the school.

Schools-within-schools offer young adolescents a stable clustering of teachers and peers. The house creates the conditions for teams of teachers and students to coalesce, for the advisor and student to get to know each other, and for students to begin to form close associations with their peers.

FORMING TEACHERS AND STUDENTS INTO TEAMS

MOST MIDDLE GRADE SCHOOLS ARE organized by academic department. Teachers' relationships with students are fragmented; math teachers see math students, history teachers see history students, and so on. Rarely, if ever, do teachers have the opportunity to develop an understanding of students as individuals, a prerequisite to teaching them well.

A better approach is to create teams of teachers and students who work together to achieve academic and personal goals for students. Teachers share responsibility for the same students and can solve problems together, often before they reach the crisis stage; teachers report that classroom discipline problems are dramatically reduced through teaming. This community of learning nurtures bonds between teacher and student that are the building blocks of the education of the young adolescent.

Teaming provides an environment conducive to learning by reducing the stress of anonymity and isolation on students.[34] Common planning by teachers of different subjects enables students to sense consistent expectations for them and to strive to meet clearly understood standards of achievement. Teaming creates the kind of learning environment that

In some aspects, Timilty Middle School is typical among Boston's schools: Its American flag has only 48 stars, several teachers lack desks, and the building, while clean, looks down at the heels. Assigned by where they live, the 500 students, 90 percent of whom are Black or Hispanic, face the struggles of many urban adolescents: peer pressure, pregnancy, drugs, family crises, and poverty.

However, Timilty is part of an experimental program in team teaching called Project Promise that has brought important changes to the school since the spring of 1985. The normal school day is extended from 1:40 to 3:10 Monday through Thursday. There is also a half-day Saturday program, increased pay for teachers selected to participate in the program by the building principal (21 of 27 were already Timilty teachers), and team teaching as a core organizational change.

The students and teachers at Timilty are divided into four teams. At the beginning of the school year, a team of 7 to 9 teachers is assigned 100 to 150 students, ensuring smaller class sizes than in non-Project Promise schools. Teachers on the teams make all academic and organizational decisions about who will teach which group of students when; how many periods of reading, mathematics, and other subjects there will be; and how long each period will last. The teachers adjust the daily schedule of classes frequently to accommodate instructional needs or special events.

The most important task of the team is to coordinate instruction. Timilty has adopted an interdisciplinary approach that emphasizes the development of communication skills. Each instructor teaches some reading, writing, and mathematics, regardless of his or her specialty. Students experience continuity in subject matter from class to class: When the social studies teacher is explaining the Bill of Rights, the English teacher has students read about Revolutionary War heros and the mathematics teacher assigns problems related to the cost of the Constitutional Convention.

At Timilty, teachers have ample time for planning, an essential element in teaming. Teams meet nearly every day for about 45 minutes at 3:10 when students leave, and for 2 hours on Friday afternoon. At team meetings, the teachers agree on what skill to emphasize. If, for example, the emphasis is on topic sentences and supporting details, every teacher in every class will ask students to find topic sentences and the supporting details. Timilty students may cover fewer of Boston's required curriculum objectives in various subjects, but the teachers are convinced that their students learn more of the needed skills. Improving the quality of the learning experience, they claim, is more important than covering all the curriculum superficially.

Taking charge of what students are taught as a team has given Timilty teachers more pleasure in their work than most of them have ever known. Along with the additional time for instruction and other elements of Project Promise, teaming has contributed to impressive gains in student achievement in its first year of implementation. In 1987, when standardized test scores across the city went up an average of 8 percentile points, Timilty's scores, although still low, went up 17 points in the 6th grade, 19 in the 7th, and 7 in the 8th. Students wrote an average of 60 papers, in draft and then final form, an unheard-of number for middle and even high schools in Boston or almost anywhere else.

Teaming at Timilty is one of the keys to a school that works.

This account is based, in part, on a Boston Globe *article of September 27, 1987.*

encourages students to grapple with ideas that may span several disciplines, and to create solutions to problems that reflect understanding, not memorization.

Interdisciplinary teams also provide a much-needed support group for teachers, eliminating the isolation teachers can experience in departmentalized settings. Morale among teachers often increases significantly with team teaching.

Teacher teams should be interdisciplinary to ensure coordination across all aspects of the core instructional program. Teachers of elective courses, special education teachers, and support staff may also be included on a team.

Two other aspects of teaming are critical. First, to foster continuity of relations and to create the learning climate students need to delve deeply into complex ideas, teams of students and teachers would preferably remain together for students' entire middle grade experience. Such arrangements promote greater understanding between and among teachers, students, and parents.

Second, so that teachers can know students on the team well, each team must have sufficient staff and the number of students on the team should be as small as possible. A team of 125 students, for example, should have a minimum of 5 teachers. Large, understaffed teams effectively end the likelihood of cultivating close, personal relations between students and teacher, and greatly reduce the value of teaming.

ASSIGNING AN ADULT ADVISOR
TO EACH STUDENT

IT IS COMMON FOR GUIDANCE counselors in middle grade schools in this country to be responsible for 500 or more students.[35] Guidance counselors are valuable members of school staffs, but reliance on a few counselors in a huge middle grade school amounts to a failed solution to a critical problem. Students do not receive the guidance they need, and counselors spread their talents and training impossibly thin.

Every student should be well known by at least one adult. Students should be able to rely on that adult to help learn from their experiences, comprehend physical changes and changing relations with family and peers, act on their behalf to marshal every school and community resource needed for the student to succeed, and help to fashion a promising vision of the future.

Small-group advisories, homerooms, or other arrangements enable teachers or other staff to provide guidance and actively monitor the academic and social development of students. Advisors should receive pre- and in-service education in adolescent development and principles of guidance. However, they would not engage in formal counseling, which would be left to a mental health professional, but would become mentors to and advocates for their students. Advisors would also serve as the primary contact between the school and parents.

Guidance counselors would retain a central role in assisting advisors in developing group activities for the advisory period, consulting with

ADVISORS AND STUDENTS BUILD RELATIONSHIPS OF TRUST

A young person entering a middle grade school for the first time needs to feel a sense of belonging, of being able to form bonds with teachers and classmates and to trust adults. Too often, the entering student feels alienated, alone, and suspicious of adults. Thus, when planners and parents designed the Shoreham-Wading River Middle School on Long Island 17 years ago, they created an advisory system that assigns an adult advisor-advocate to each student. The system has become the core organizing principle of the school.

The ratio of advisors to students is never more than 1 adult for 10 students. To maintain small advisory groups, virtually all school staff, including administrative, art, health, physical education, and library staff and even the principal, serve as advisors.

Advisories start the day. The advisor meets with his or her group for 10 minutes before classes begin to discuss school issues and students' activities. This session, similar to the familiar homeroom period, sends the students off to class from a secure and stable base. Students and their advisors meet later in the day for 15 minutes to eat lunch together.

Advisors meet twice a month before classes begin with each student on a one-to-one basis or in small groups. Two bus runs each morning ensure that students scheduled for a pre-class session can get to school. The sessions offer a chance to discuss academics, projects, home or school problems, or anything that interests the student and advisor. When a student seems uneasy in the one-to-one setting, the advisor may suggest bringing a friend for support.

The advisor, assigned to the student for the entire year, observes the student both in classes and in after-school activities and discusses the student with other staff and faculty. The student gets to know this one adult well, and learns that there is at least one person at the school with the time to hear out the student's side of things. If the student misbehaves, for example, the principal consults the advisor before deciding if punishment is called for, and the advisor may, after discussing the case with the student, suggest alternative treatment.

Advisors also meet twice a year with parents to discuss the student's grades and progress in school. Teachers send all grades and comments to the advisor, who collates the information, enters it on the report card, and discusses the student with the parents. Individual parents' meetings with advisors are attended by 98 percent of the parents.

The advisors, for their part, do not try to become amateur therapists. The guidance counselor and psychologist train and support all advisors and offer specific recommendations for handling particular problems.

The Shoreham-Wading advisory system includes every student, not just those who demand attention or earn special recognition. The system makes it possible for a young person to develop a supportive relationship with an adult who is not a parent. The system ensures that each student has access to a trustworthy adult with whom the student can communicate and share ideas and concerns.

The effect of the advisory system appears to be to reduce alienation of students and to provide each young adolescent with the support of a caring adult who knows that student well. That bond can make the student's engagement and interest in learning a reality.

advisors on students' problems, counseling students with problems that go beyond what the advisors are trained to handle, and connecting students to appropriate community resources when the school cannot adequately meet a youth's need.

TEACHING A CORE OF COMMON KNOWLEDGE

Every student in the middle grades should learn to think critically through mastery of an appropriate body of knowledge, lead a healthy life, behave ethically and lawfully, and assume the responsibilities of citizenship in a pluralistic society.

EVERY MIDDLE GRADE SCHOOL should offer a core academic program and should expect every student to complete that program successfully. The purpose of setting this goal is practical: The future of this nation as a stable, prosperous democracy requires that all members contribute to the common good of society and meet their obligations as citizens.

The broad outlines of the curriculum are the responsibility of state and local school authorities. But middle grade educators can fashion a full academic program for all students that integrates English, fine arts, foreign languages, history, literature and grammar, mathematics, science, and social studies.

A curriculum containing these subjects today frequently lacks depth. At best, students are asked to demonstrate competency in the subject matter, but not in the ability to think or express themselves about topics that range across each subject. Middle grade schools, in conjunction with state and local authorities, can vastly improve middle grade curricula and instruction programs by:

▲ Teaching young adolescents to think critically;

▲ Teaching young adolescents to develop healthful lifestyles;

▲ Teaching young adolescents to be active citizens;

▲ Integrating subject matter across disciplines; and

▲ Teaching students to learn as well as to test successfully.

TEACHING YOUNG ADOLESCENTS TO THINK CRITICALLY

MANY MIDDLE GRADE SCHOOLS IN this country fail to support and challenge youth. Nowhere is this failure more evident than in the development of American young adolescents' critical reasoning and higher order thinking.*

Contrary to much conventional belief, cognitive development during early adolescence is not on hold. Belief in such claims has had substantial and damaging effects on middle grade education, by limiting innovation in curriculum development that might require new and more advanced ways of thinking. A thorough review of recent studies on adolescent cognitive development found "no persuasive evidence" that young adolescents cannot engage in critical and higher order thinking.[37]

A primary goal in choosing curricula and teaching methods in the middle grades should be the disciplining of young adolescents' minds, that is, their capacity for active, engaged thinking. A student with a disciplined mind can assimilate knowledge, rather than merely recall information by rote or apply simple algorithms. The student can challenge the reliability of evidence; recognize the viewpoint or voice behind the words, pictures, or ideas presented; see relationships between ideas; and ask what-if and suppose-that questions.

A disciplined mind connotes a disposition toward inquiry, discovery, and reasoning across all subjects. A student cannot, of course, develop a disciplined mind apart from specific subject matter. The key lies in how the student approaches the subject matter. In the traditional curriculum, the student learns subject by subject. This fragmented array does not allow students to connect new and old ideas or to construct their own meaning of the information.

In the core curriculum of the transformed middle grade school, the student confronts themes, which are clusters of subjects, and learns to inquire, associate, and synthesize across subjects. The student learns to reason even while absorbing basic information about the subject matter. This approach clearly requires that the current emphasis on coverage of a large quantity of information must yield to an emphasis on depth or quality of the student's understanding. Schools can choose the most important principles and concepts within each subject, and concentrate instruction there.

Developing a discipline of mind requires a radical departure from traditional classroom instruction. Above all, it requires a shift in long-held beliefs that the role of teachers is to transmit knowledge to students. Instead, teachers must view themselves as facilitators through which young people construct knowledge themselves. Teachers will need the support of administrators in their new role.

Teachers will be called upon to promote a spirit of inquiry and to stimulate students to think about and communicate ideas. Far greater reliance will be placed on learning techniques that allow students to participate actively in discovering and creating new solutions to problems.

For example, young adolescents need group approaches to learning. Learning often takes place best when students have opportunities to discuss, analyze, express opinions, and receive feedback from peers.[38] Peer involvement is especially critical during early adolescence when the influence of peers increases and becomes more important to the young person.

*Higher order thinking is difficult to define. Resnick has identified the following characteristics: Higher order thinking is nonalgorithmic (the path of action is not fully specified in advance); tends to be complex, involving multiple perspectives; often yields multiple rather than unique solutions; involves dealing with uncertainty and gaps in information; involves the application of multiple, sometimes conflicting criteria; is self-regulating; and involves considerable mental effort.[36]

E D U C A T O R S   O F   Y O U N G   A D O L E S C E N T S need to reconsider the contemporary approach to health education, which treats health education as a requirement of minor importance. Teachers of health education are too often not trained in the subject and devote little time to it.

One solution in middle grades is the integration of health education

The landmark report, *Project 2061: Science For All Americans*, published by the American Association for the Advancement of Science (AAAS), presents recommendations on the scientific knowledge, skills, and attitudes that all students should acquire in their education from kindergarten through high school. Recommendations cover:

▲ The Nature of Science
▲ The Nature of Mathematics
▲ The Nature of Technology
▲ The Physical Setting
▲ The Living Environment
▲ The Human Organism
▲ Human Society
▲ The Designed World
▲ The Mathematical World
▲ Historical Perspectives
▲ Common Themes
▲ Habits of Mind

Many of these topics are already represented in school curricula. But the AAAS scientific panels recommend coverage that differs fundamentally from current practice.

First, boundaries between academic disciplines should be reduced and linkages among them emphasized. The basic principles involved in the transformations of energy, for example, can be illustrated in the study of physical and biological sciences and technological systems. The concept of evolution is demonstrable in stars, organisms, and societies.

Second, students need to memorize considerably fewer facts than in traditional science, mathematics, and technology courses. Ideas and thinking skills are emphasized over specialized vocabulary and memorized procedures.

The effective teaching of science, mathematics, and technology must be based on learning principles that derive from systematic research and from well-tested practice, the report says. It urges teachers to consider the following:

▲ *Start with questions about nature.* Sound teaching begins with phenomena and questions that are interesting and familiar to students, not with phenomena or abstractions outside the range of experience, understanding, or knowledge.

▲ *Engage students actively.* Students need to have many and varied opportunities for collecting, sorting, and cataloging; observing, notetaking, and sketching; interviewing, polling, and surveying; using hand lenses, microscopes, thermometers, cameras, and other common instruments; measuring, counting, and computing; and systematically observing the social behavior of humans and other animals.

▲ *Concentrate on the collection and use of evidence.* Students should be challenged with problems, at levels appropriate to their maturity, that require them to decide what evidence is relevant to the solution and to interpret for themselves what the evidence means.

▲ *Provide historical perspectives.* During their school years, students should encounter many scientific ideas presented in their historical context.

▲ *Insist on clear expression.* Teachers should place a high priority on effective oral and written communication for all students.

▲ *Use a team approach.* The collaborative nature of scientific work should be strongly reinforced by frequent group activity in the classroom.

▲ *Do not separate knowing from finding out.* In science, conclusions and methods that lead to them are tightly coupled. The nature of inquiry depends on what is being investigated, and what is learned depends on the methods used.

▲ *Deemphasize the memorization of technical vocabulary.* Understanding rather than vocabulary should be the main purpose of teaching science.

into the core instructional program as an element of the life sciences. Students who learn about health within the context of the life sciences find out about how their bodies grow and function. They come to realize the value of a healthful diet and exercise while recognizing the dangers of illicit drugs, alcohol, and tobacco.

A premier example of the integration of health and the life sciences can be found in the Human Biology Program at Stanford University. This highly successful interdisciplinary undergraduate major integrates the biological and behavioral sciences. Stanford educators are now adapting it from postsecondary education to the middle grades.

Life sciences education alone is unlikely to persuade young people to reject self-destructive or dangerous behavior. Young people need training in skills that help them to resist interpersonal or media messages to engage in specific negative behaviors, increase self-control and self-esteem, reduce stress and anxiety, gain in the ability to express apprehension and disapproval, and become assertive. These abilities are often referred to as life skills.

Students can learn these essential life skills through systematic instruction and role-playing. Efforts to teach adolescents these skills have been effective in preventing adolescent smoking[39] and substance abuse.[40] An intervention based on life skill development has also been effective in preventing pregnancies among older adolescents,[41] although its effectiveness in preventing sexual activity and pregnancy among young adolescents has not yet been evaluated.

As young people learn about their health and how to avoid problem behaviors, they must also gain access to health care and be able to exercise options in selecting care, important issues discussed later in this report.

EARLY ADOLESCENCE OFFERS A superb opportunity to learn values, skills, and a sense of social responsibility important for citizenship in the United States. Every middle grade school should include youth service — supervised activity helping others in the community or in school — in its core instructional program.

Youth service can teach young people about values for full participation in this society. Educators agree that their mission includes teaching values for citizenship. These values certainly include compassion, regard for human worth and dignity, respect for others' rights, tolerance and appreciation of human diversity, willingness to cooperate, and a desire for social justice.

Youth service also teaches students about collaboration, problem-solving, conflict resolution, and seeing projects in their entirety rather than in pieces. These skills are essential in the workplace.[42] Consequently, middle grade schools should look upon youth service as central to the academic program.

Service opportunities abound within the middle grade school itself. Students can serve as peer and cross-age tutors, teaching assistants, lab

Early adolescence provides unprecedented opportunities for science education to capitalize on the natural curiosity about bodily changes and to adopt more healthful lifestyles. By the same token, it is during adolescence that young people may engage in self-damaging behaviors that may shorten life or worsen it.

A promising example of using life sciences curriculum to teach healthy behavior is the Human Biology Program at Stanford University, a highly successful interdisciplinary undergraduate major that integrates the biological and behavioral sciences. This university program is now being adapted to the middle grades as a two-year curriculum (grades 7 and 8) aimed at capturing the interest of young adolescents in the study of biology through learning about themselves and others.

A comprehensive life sciences curriculum can teach middle grade students essential concepts in biology and behavior, and then relate these concepts to high-risk behaviors and health hazards that students encounter in their daily lives: pregnancy, sexually transmitted diseases, alcohol, drugs, and eating disorders. Thus, improvement of science education in the middle grades is expected to capture the attention of more 10- to 15-year-olds in the study of science than do current approaches.

The Middle Grades Life Sciences Curriculum begins by describing the nature of adolescent development, focusing on the biological underpinnings and social responses to puberty. It moves directly to sexuality: the reproductive system, sexual behavior, and maintaining health. Because of their central importance in the lives of young adolescent, subjects take up the entir. urst semester of the first year. The second semester of the first year deals with the concept of culture, including marriage and the family in the American and other societies.

The second year focuses on the physiology of body systems, their behavioral associations, implications for good health, and societal consequences.

The Middle Grades Life Sciences Curriculum is a prime example of an interdisciplinary core curriculum, including texts, resources, and teacher materials, that integrates the life sciences with health education and health promotion.

assistants, safety officers, school governance committee members, student court officers, assistants in coordinating youth service, and in many other roles. Youth service can expand beyond the boundaries of the school. Students who assist in childcare, help the handicapped, clean up a debris-strewn stream, or advocate for the homeless are assuming meaningful roles and responding to real problems. Integrating service into the core curriculum enables teachers to tie classroom instruction to real-life, hands-on learning experiences within the community.

Fully integrating youth service into the core program will require new roles for teachers and administrators to establish and coordinate youth-service opportunities. Teachers will need to provide opportunities for students to reflect on and learn from their service experience. Additional personnel, community service coordinators, may be needed to arrange student placements, coordinate with site supervisors, and oversee students' service activities on campus. The community can be expected to respond affirmatively to youth service, which offers many opportunities for partnerships with community organizations. Many youth organizations have long traditions of involving young people in

VALUED YOUTH: POTENTIAL DROPOUTS SERVE AS TUTORS

In San Antonio, 45 percent of Hispanic students drop out of school before graduating from high school; more than half of these youth leave before 9th grade. To stop this loss, the Intercultural Development and Research Association (IDRA), a local organization, designed the Valued Youth Partnership Program to engage potential dropouts, train them as tutors, and assign each tutor to three to five students at adjacent elementary schools.

The rationale for the program is two-fold. First, IDRA research determined that teachers could spot students at risk for dropping out through a combination of declining grades, rising absenteeism, and increasing behavior problems. Second, review of numerous studies of cross-age tutoring showed that tutors made significant gains in achievement, even greater than did tutees.

The Valued Youth Program was launched with funding from a local Coca Cola Bottling Company for pilot programs, development of models and training materials, and evaluation.

Currently about 150 Valued Youth from 5 San Antonio middle schools (two school districts) tutor 4 to 8 hours a week. Boys and girls participate in equal numbers.

A rise in tutors' self-esteem is the most noticeable effect of the program, according to IDRA. As a result, only 2 percent of all tutors have dropped out of school. This is remarkable, given that all of these students had been held back twice or more and were reading at least two grade levels below their current grade placement. Disciplinary problems have become less severe, grades have improved, and attendance of tutors has soared.

In addition to tutoring, students learn problem-solving and the value of speaking to others respectfully. They also hear guest speakers, often successful community leaders who attended the same school or grew up in the neighborhood, describe career options. Recognition ceremonies, with tee shirts and rewards, give the tutors status at school and in their community.

Valued Youth confirms that tutors often gain more than tutees: By teaching, one learns; by giving, one grows.

---

service, both in the community and at their agencies, and are natural partners with middle grade schools for such a program.

In concert with the youth service program, schools must reflect the values they teach. An ethic of mutual respect must pervade the school, in the way school staff treat students and in the way staff treat each other. Appreciation of cultural diversity, application of equal opportunity practices, and sensitivity to ethnic and racial pluralism within the community should be reflected in the composition of the school staff, which in many schools will require the hiring of more minority teachers.

YOUNG ADOLESCENTS DEMONSTRATE an ability to grapple with complexity, think critically, and deal with information as parts of systems rather than as isolated, disconnected facts. Currently, middle grade curricula package ideas and information strictly by subject, making it difficult for students to see connections between ideas in different disciplines,

INTEGRATING SUBJECT MATTER
ACROSS DISCIPLINES

The core middle grade curriculum can be organized around integrating themes that young people find relevant to their own lives. For example, separate courses in English, arts, history, and social studies might be grouped into the humanities, organized around an integrating theme such as Immigration. Mathematics and science could be combined in the study of themes such as Mapping the Environment.

The core program can capitalize on young adolescents' concerns and curiosity about their own physical and emotional development and their place within the family, peer group, and larger society. Thus the life sciences, which link biology, physiology, genetics, human evolution, and behavior to health education, could be clustered around themes relating to the developing adolescent. Young adolescents are also increasingly concerned about fairness and justice. An interdisciplinary focus on the Struggle for Freedom in America would enable them to explore these subjects in depth.

Interdisciplinary themes can also enhance young people's recognition that the United States is now a part of a global economy and an interdependent society of nations, and that the composition of our own population is racially and ethnically increasingly diverse. Themes that explore human diversity offer one way of dealing positively with what may become a source of social unrest in this nation as the relative size of minority groups increases in coming years.

TEACHING STUDENTS TO LEARN AS WELL AS TO TEST SUCCESSFULLY

IN AMERICAN EDUCATION, THE assessment of student performance inordinately influences curriculum and methods of instruction. From kindergarten to graduate school, educators teach to the test.

The transformed middle grade school will require new assessment approaches, which are being developed today.[43] In a transformed middle grade school, all forms of student assessment would reflect the purposes of instruction as described in this report. For example, curriculum and teaching methods should promote disciplined inquiry among young adolescents. If higher order or critical thinking is not being assessed, teachers are less likely to demand it of students.[44]

In the transformed middle grade school, tests will more closely resemble real learning tasks. One example is long-term writing assignments that emphasize the development of ideas and coherent expression. A student's written product represents important learning, not memorization, and practice for the test is practice with real writing.[45] Individual and group projects also offer students opportunities to exhibit their knowledge of a subject or issue in a way that is meaningful to them. Problems in mathematics or science that have alternate solutions further represent the kinds of activities that require students to demonstrate a full range of thinking skills, and assimilate ideas and information across subjects.

State and national achievement tests will also differ from current practice. One promising alternative is to assess student performance on the basis of work portfolios as well as of test scores. For example, student achievement in writing and mathematics could be determined partly on the basis of standardized tests measuring state objectives, and partly on examples of students' best work as determined by the youth and their teachers. Such a procedure would establish a direct link between statewide assessment procedures and classroom activities in individual schools.[46]

All young adolescents should have the opportunity to succeed in every aspect of the middle grade program, regardless of previous achievement or the pace at which they learn.

ENSURING SUCCESS FOR ALL STUDENTS

THIS REPORT CALLS FOR EVERY MIDDLE grade student to complete the core instructional program successfully. Ensuring success for all students should be adopted by transformed middle grade schools as an attainable goal, not a slogan. Middle grade schools must increase their success rates dramatically. Schools must encourage students who fall short of success to try again and again, and schools must try again and again, using every means available, to see that all students succeed.

Completion of the core instructional program, however, should not be the only criterion of a successful middle grade experience. Middle grade schools must strive to offer each student opportunities to exhibit excellence and to gain the confidence and personal satisfaction of becoming expert or very good at something. For many young people, mastering the core academic program will provide these opportunities. For others, opportunities to exhibit excellence may lie outside the core program in exploratory courses or athletics, or outside the schoolhouse through youth service or other community-based activities.

To ensure that all students learn, the educational program must be shaped to fit the needs of students by:
▲ Grouping students for learning;
▲ Scheduling classroom periods to maximize learning; and
▲ Expanding the structure of opportunity for learning.

GROUPING STUDENTS BY CLASSES according to achievement level is almost universal in middle grade schools.[47] In theory, this between-class "tracking" reduces the heterogeneity of the class and enables teachers to adjust instruction to students' knowledge and skills. Greater achievement is then possible for both "low-" and "high-ability" students.

In practice, this kind of tracking has proven to be one of the most divisive and damaging school practices in existence. Time and again, young people placed in lower academic tracks or classes, often during the

GROUPING STUDENTS FOR LEARNING

middle grades, are locked into dull, repetitive instructional programs leading at best to minimum competencies. The psychic numbing these youth experience from a "dumbed-down" curriculum contrasts sharply with the exciting opportunities for learning and critical thinking that students in the higher tracks or classes may experience.[48]

Once placed in lower tracks, students often do not move up. While lower track youth refine basic skills, students in higher tracks move to more advanced ones. The gap in achievement between "low-ability" and "high-ability" students widens, and isolation between the two groups increases.[49] While tracking is potentially harmful to virtually all young people, it is particularly damaging if a student is placed in a lower track on all subjects based on ability in one major academic area. Then the student cannot succeed in areas of higher ability either, and is locked into low stimulation throughout the curriculum and over the years. Being locked into a lower track over several school years and many subjects is likely to restrict opportunity as an adult.

Because minority youth are disproportionately placed in lower academic groups,[50] tracking often serves to reinforce racial isolation in schools, helps to perpetuate racial prejudice among students, and may increase alienation toward school among lower achieving students. This consequence is especially damaging in the middle grades, when young people's impressions regarding the value of those racially and culturally different from themselves begin to become entrenched. Despite this long-term harm to students who are restricted to lower tracks, tracking remains a pervasive method for organizing instruction in middle grade schools.

The challenge, then, is to focus once again on the goal that tracking sought to achieve in the first place: effectively teaching students of diverse ability and differing rates of learning. Two well-documented approaches have emerged in the past several decades that achieve this goal: cooperative learning and cross-age tutoring.

In cooperative learning situations, all students contribute to the group effort because students receive group rewards as well as individual grades. High achievers deepen their understanding of material by explaining it to lower achievers; those of lower achievement receive immediate tutoring from their peers and gain a sense of accomplishment by suggesting solutions to problems.[51]

Cooperative learning has been shown to help students to learn course material faster and retain it longer and to develop critical reasoning power more rapidly than working alone.[52] Cooperative learning also requires students to get to know and work with classmates of different ethnic, racial, and cultural backgrounds, setting the stage for requirements of adult work life and for citizenship in a multi-cultural society.[53] Students in cooperative settings tend to accept disabled classmates more readily than they do in other settings.[54]

While cooperative learning is one way to ensure greater success, cross-age tutoring is another. A multi-grade sub-school or house in the transformed middle grade school lends itself to cross-age tutoring, which casts older students in the role of teaching younger students and is a

MATHEMATICS STUDENTS COOPERATE TO ACCELERATE

Steve Parsons, an 8th grade mathematics teacher at West Frederick (Maryland) Middle School, has used cooperative learning techniques for 13 years, primarily to accelerate learning among low mathematics achievers. Parsons is currently using a cooperative learning curriculum developed at The Johns Hopkins University called Team Accelerated Instruction (TAI).

Students in TAI work together to obtain individual and group rewards. Students are pre-tested to determine their current level of mathematics achievement and receive a textbook based on their score. Students are then grouped into teaching teams and home teams. Teaching teams consist of students who scored at about the same level on the achievement test and were assigned the same text. Home teams are made up of four students, one with a relatively high pre-test achievement score, two with average scores, and one with a low score.

A typical TAI session follows a pattern. Students on the same teaching team are pulled out from their home teams to receive about 20 minutes of instruction on a new unit in the text focusing on several related mathematical concepts or skills. Students then return to their home teams and work on problems in the text, checking their answers with teammates. When students have trouble with problems, teammates help them to analyze the problems, thus providing immediate tutoring while the teacher continues to work with other teaching teams. Students eventually are tested for individual grades and earn points for their home team. Teaching teams are constantly re-formed as students progress to higher levels of ability.

All students are taught the importance of encouraging others and working together to solve mathematical problems. Students are often initially uncertain that they really will be rewarded for working together, but are soon convinced and quickly come to enjoy being able to learn from each other "even if all the talk is about math," Parsons says. "Students say they love math class because they don't have to do any work," he says, "yet these same students are passing the tests and mastering material at an accelerated pace."

Five major research studies conducted by Hopkins researchers involving more than 3,000 public school students document the effectiveness of TAI. In those studies, TAI students consistently showed a 2-to-1 ratio in achievement gains over control students.

Parsons, working with special education teachers, has also had considerable success with TAI and other cooperative learning techniques in mainstreaming special education students who had been placed in an extremely low-ability mathematics track. These youth, some of whom had severe emotional problems, gained the acceptance and aid of many of their peers, progressed through the series of TAI tests at mastery level, and functioned at a more mature level in the classroom.

Based, in part, on these successes, Frederick County school officials are moving toward eliminating the special education mathematics track as well as other achievement-based tracks that currently exist. This move will begin with several pilot efforts in the fall of 1989. Teachers involved in these trials will receive extensive training in cooperative education techniques for effectively teaching heterogeneous groups of students. The county school board is also planning to hire a full-time cooperative education specialist to train teachers throughout the district.

proven method of providing additional support for students who need it. Cross-age tutoring could take place, for example, during the part of the day reserved for activities outside the core instructional program for younger and older students. Cross-age tutoring has shown consistent positive effects on achievement outcomes for both tutors and tutees.[55] Tutors encounter opportunities to review basic skills without embarrassment, gain experience in applying academic abilities, and develop insight into the process of teaching and learning. Tutees receive individualized instruction and work with positive role models.

Strong evidence exists that students at every level of achievement can be effective tutors.[56] Low achievers can demonstrate that they are capable of learning and helping others to learn. High achievers develop a sense of responsibility for those less advanced.

SCHEDULING CLASSROOM PERIODS TO MAXIMIZE LEARNING

STUDENTS NEED TIME TO LEARN, especially to learn material in depth. When the time alloted for classes is always limited to 40 or 50 minutes, many youth will not master all the material.

A key feature of the transformed middle grade school should be flexibility in the duration of classes. Teacher teams should be able to change class schedules whenever, in their collective professional judgment, the need exists. They should be able to create blocks of time for instruction that best meets the needs and interests of the students, responds to curriculum priorities, and capitalizes on learning opportunities such as current events.

EXPANDING THE STRUCTURE OF OPPORTUNITY FOR LEARNING

CHANGES IN CURRICULUM, INSTRUCtion, organization, and scheduling will vastly increase the odds of success for every young adolescent. Realistically, some students, perhaps many, will need more help, particularly if expectations for their success are raised. Indeed, higher expectations, alone, will not improve performance unless accompanied by individual attention, strong teacher involvement, and before- and after-school learning opportunities.

Each middle school needs a plan for "continuous correction" to provide additional support for students needing more time, encouragement, or instruction to learn.[57] This plan may require extending the school day, providing summer school or Saturday enrichment programs, specialized daily instruction, greater involvement of the home in learning activities, or combinations of these, depending upon a student's individual needs.

Expanding opportunities for learning should not be taken to mean only greater remedial education for "slow learners." One of the greatest failures of the current educational system is that youth for whom some lessons come hard are regarded as generally incompetent. It is simply not true that students who have to work the hardest in one subject area will

LOUIS ARMSTRONG MIDDLE SCHOOL: A COMMUNITY LEARNING CENTER

Learning knows few boundaries at the Louis Armstrong Middle School in the Queens borough of New York City. Through linkages to community organizations and a local college, and by setting aside traditional limits on when and where education can occur, Armstrong serves the educational needs of its students and the surrounding community.

Although no bus service is provided before regular classes begin, the Early Bird program attracts about 300 of the 1,300 students from throughout Queens who are enrolled at Armstrong. The program provides 40 minutes of sports, music (especially jazz), computers, foreign language, and crafts. In one popular Early Bird class, students develop their own radio programs for broadcast over the school's public address system. Early Bird teachers are primarily Queens College interns, although parents and teachers also provide instruction.

After school, from 3:30 to 5:30, a community-based organization called Elmcore tutors students, in the school building, who need extra help. Young people are referred to the program by teachers, or choose to attend on their own. Elmcore also offers computer seminars, dance classes, and sports programs.

Saturday morning classes draw about 200 students from two dozen Queens public schools and nine parochial schools. Regular teachers and Queens College interns offer two-and-one-half-hour classes in computers, pantomime, writing, and a joint child-parent art workshop.

During the summer, a program for teachers called Ways of Knowing explores how specialists, such as historians, mathematicians, and scientists, conduct their inquiries. Teachers conduct workshops for their colleagues on this approach to helping students learn how people discover and create knowledge.

Armstrong also opens its doors to individuals in the community in need of further education. About 100 adults, mostly from the large Colombian community near the school, study English as a second language (ESL) at the school during the day. Classes for students earning high school equivalency degrees and ESL are taught at night. Often, students in ESL night courses bring their parents to learn together.

As Armstrong supports the community, the community supports Armstrong. For example, the community provides an array of youth service opportunities for Armstrong students. About 40 students report for work in non-profit service agencies, at nearby LaGuardia Airport, in TV and radio repair shops, and at the local police precinct. The Lincoln Center Institute and the Museum Collaborative both offer visiting artist programs for teachers and students.

At Louis Armstrong Middle School, the doors are always open for learning.

necessarily be the least competent in another. A student struggling in mathematics may excel in language arts. Moreover, because variability is the hallmark of early adolescence, some youth may advance rapidly and suddenly after years of struggling. One way to avoid labeling extra "after-school" time for academic subjects solely as "remedial" and as punishment is to provide similar after-school enrichment in less traditional academic areas. Thereby, students can increase skills in a wide variety of areas, according to individual needs.

Thus, middle grade schools should strive to create a structure of opportunities for learning that nourishes the strengths and overcomes the weaknesses of individual students. A school's plan to develop such a structure might require new responsibilities for teachers and administrators, greater resources, and significant new institutional arrangements involving labor unions and others to ensure that schools are accessible and safe at all times when the program is operating. The existence of such opportunities across the country shows that schools can create expanded structures for learning.

EMPOWERING TEACHERS AND ADMINISTRATORS

Decisions concerning the experiences of middle grade students should be made by the adults who know them best.

DEEPLY INGRAINED IN OUR SOCIETY is the belief that individuals can be trusted to make decisions for themselves and for the common good. This belief is the bedrock of the democratic political system. Increasingly, it is being adapted in business and industry as a means of involving employees in decisions about their work. Business managers find that empowering workers to decide on a wide range of issues affecting them increases their productivity, improves the quality of their work, and heightens their morale.

Democratization may be entering the American workplace, but it has not yet penetrated American public education. Teachers and administrators in middle grade schools today are, as in all levels of American elementary and secondary education, severely limited in their ability to make key decisions regarding their own professional practice.

Teachers must have greater authority to make decisions, and responsibility for the consequences of those decisions, regarding the day-to-day educational experiences of their students. Dramatically improved outcomes for young adolescents require individualized, responsive, and creative approaches to teaching that will occur only when teachers are able to use their intimate knowledge of students to design instructional programs. Moreover, teachers need the opportunity to bring their own special interests and expertise to their teaching. Young people exposed to ideas about which teachers care deeply see course material not as isolated facts and abstract concepts, but as powerful forces that affect people's lives and arouse people's passions.

More importantly, students who witness teachers making decisions and discussing important ideas can envision what it is like to participate in decisionmaking. Increasingly, they can become a part of decisions affecting their education. Young adolescents yearn for responsibility, independence, and self-direction. Yet research on American junior high schools shows that students appear to have fewer opportunities for making decisions than in elementary schools, a perception that both students and teachers share.[58]

Students should begin in middle grade school to feel that they are part of a responsive educational system in which they have defined rights and clear responsibilities. The empowerment of school staff is a necessary and desirable step in creating a transformed middle grade school that produces responsible, ethical, and participating future citizens. Middle grade schools can achieve these objectives by:

- ▲ Giving teachers greater influence in the classroom;
- ▲ Establishing building governance committees; and
- ▲ Designating leaders for the teaching process.

TEACHERS ON TEAMS SHOULD EXERCISE creative control over how curricular goals are to be reached for their team. Teachers should collectively allocate budget and space for the team, choose instructional methods and materials for classroom use, identify and develop interdisciplinary curricular themes, schedule classes, select field experiences including youth service opportunities, and evaluate students' performance in light of school-wide objectives. Teachers on teams should also have a significant voice in recruiting new teachers for the team or within the house.

Teachers need time to form themselves into smoothly functioning teams. They need time to plan all aspects of implementing the transformation process — how they will introduce cooperative learning and when they will use hands-on instruction, for example. They need time during the school day to work out schedules and make adjustments in the daily program. They need time to express ideas, talk about students for whom they share responsibility, describe their successes to other teachers, and seek counsel from colleagues on solving problems.

Empowering teachers to design courses has important implications for evaluating their effectiveness. Teachers will be working in teams and the teams will be responsible for shaping individualized academic programs for students. In exchange for thus empowering teams of teachers, it is reasonable to expect those teams to assume greater responsibility for how well their students perform.

CREATIVE CONTROL OF YOUNG people's educational experiences should clearly be the responsibility of teachers on teams within the relatively small school-within-school structure. Effective management of other aspects of the educational program involving all houses or sub-schools requires building-wide structures for shared decisionmaking.

A building governance committee can invite representatives of each sub-school community — teachers, administrators, support staff, parents, students, and key representatives from community organizations — to participate in decisionmaking. Each house might be represented on the building governance committee by a teacher from each team within the house.

The building governance committee can serve in an advisory capacity to the building principal. To work well, the arrangement requires a genuine effort to reach consensus on issues. The principal is open-minded and willing to listen; committee members recognize that the principal has

GIVING TEACHERS GREATER
INFLUENCE IN THE CLASSROOM

ESTABLISHING BUILDING
GOVERNANCE COMMITTEES

ultimate responsibility for overall operation and performance of the building.

The jurisdiction of the building governance committee differs from that of teams of teachers, although a good deal of synergism between teams and the committee is likely to occur. The building governance committee enables all sectors of the middle grade school community to establish comprehensive goals for all students. The committee assists school staff to learn from parents and others in the community about students' family structures and kinship groups, housing, and cultural and ethnic heritage. Such information relayed to teams of teachers is critical in developing instructional programs that are sensitive to young adolescents' diverse backgrounds.

The committee coordinates and integrates all activities that occur within the school building and between school and community organizations. To the process of transforming current middle grade schools, the committee adds the essential mechanism for educators, health and social service professionals, youth organization representatives, parents, and others to initiate, plan, monitor, and evaluate new relationships and organizational structures. As such, the committee can systematically foster interaction among stakeholders in the middle grade school, interaction that promotes the trust and respect essential to the processes of change.[59]

DESIGNATING LEADERS FOR THE TEACHING PROCESS

THIS REPORT EMPHASIZES THE NEED to create smaller educational environments for young adolescents than currently exist by dividing large schools into smaller houses or sub-schools that co-exist within the same school building. This change in school organization has significant implications for the administration of middle grade schools. To accommodate the changed school organization, a new administrative position—that of house or sub-school leader—will be required, and the building principal will take on new roles.

Each school-within-school or house, of 200 to 300 but no more than 500 students, will need a leader who is directly responsible for creating an environment conducive to team teaching. This person is the lead teacher, a person who works with teams of teachers to develop ideas for curriculum, obtains needed resources for instruction, helps teams to solve problems involving individual students, and offers advice when additional support services are needed.

Picture, for example, how a house leader can help teachers on a team who want their students to have more hands-on experience in physical sciences. The house leader might contact outside resources—businesses with special laboratory facilities or a local college physics department, for instance. The leader might help teachers to identify and evaluate potential curriculum materials or computer software. The leader could also help to establish appropriate procedures to evaluate the outcomes of the new practices.

The building principal would be responsible for the safe and efficient

SCHOOL GOVERNANCE IS A TEAM EFFORT

The pervasive assumption in our society that poor school achievement is to be expected of children from low-income families was challenged and proven incorrect in a 20-year program of research headed by Dr. James P. Comer, a psychiatrist at the Yale University Child Study Center. Working in two New Haven, Connecticut, elementary schools, Comer found that many problems ascribed to students are, in fact, associated with poor relations among school staff and between those adults and parents. He established that improving these relations can lead to better governance of the school and to better performance by students.

Both elementary schools have student bodies that are nearly 100 percent Black, are largely from economically disadvantaged households, and were ranked near the bottom of all New Haven elementary schools in reading and mathematics scores. The Martin Luther King Jr. School, where the Comer plan went into effect in 1968, now ranks fifth among all New Haven schools in academic achievement and first in attendance; students at the other school, where the process went into effect in 1974, have achieved similar results.

Superintendent John Dow Jr. has now mandated the Comer plan for New Haven middle schools. The key element is the building-level School Planning and Management Team (SPMT). The SPMT is a school-wide committee composed of peer-nominated representatives of teachers, administrators, support staff, and parents who advise the principal on decisions regarding all aspects of the school's program.

The SPMT fosters good relations among staff and between staff and parents by reaching decisions through consensus rather than by voting, and by operating on the principle of no blame; attention is constantly focused on collaborative problem-solving rather than determining who is at fault. Everyone on the SPMT is encouraged to express an opinion without fear of ridicule or retribution.

The SPMT is a prime example of the creation of a community of purpose for educating young adolescents. Cooperative decision-making is extended throughout the school by involving as many staff and parents as possible in SPMT subcommittees. Each year, the SPMT and its subcommittees produce a comprehensive school plan that articulates the school's goals for students' academic and social development, social climate within the building, staff development, and public relations. "We view that plan like the Bible," says Charles Warner, principal of the Jackie Robinson Middle School. "It's like a school-site contract with teachers that everyone buys into because they created it. We're all constantly checking to see if we are following the plan."

The result, according to Warner, who was apprehensive at first in sharing his authority with staff and parents, is a significant improvement in the way staff work together. "No one is afraid to speak out on what they believe is in a student's best interest."

For students, the sense of adults pulling together for the common good and renewed responsibility for student outcomes among teachers has improved student involvement in learning, Warner says. He further observes that in the year before the Comer plan was introduced, about 17 girls attending Robinson became mothers. Three years after the program was in place, only four girls became mothers. Warner attributes this change to the fact that teachers now take time in class to concentrate on raising young people's self-respect and teaching decisionmaking skills to help youth make better choices concerning their behavior, two goals contained in the SPMT comprehensive school plan. Because the SPMT had endorsed these goals, "Teachers are not criticized for taking time to teach values" that are shared within the school.

Sharing values, goals, and dreams is what it's all about at Robinson Middle School.

functioning of the entire school. He or she would create an environment in which each house can be a truly creative enterprise. Such a principal would have some attributes now associated with superintendents of school districts: political skill at helping groups of people to solve problems, the capacity to articulate a broad educational vision, the ability to see and plan based on broader trends (e.g., changes in the population of the community and fluctuations in resources), and the capacity to understand and deal effectively with the larger civic and political context of the school, including the business community, policymakers, and the broader public. The building administrator would also be responsible for equity and fairness in allocating resources among houses, and for developing means to collect and make accessible data needed to ensure public accountability of school-wide student outcomes.

Both the house leader and building principal's jobs require considerably more freedom of action and school-site decisionmaking powers than middle grade school administrators currently possess. At both levels of leadership, these individuals will act as creative forces in shaping the educational experiences of young adolescents. This dimension will attract energetic, creative individuals to these positions.

PREPARING TEACHERS FOR THE MIDDLE GRADES

Teachers in middle grade schools should be selected and specially educated to teach young adolescents.

MANY TEACHERS OF YOUNG ADOLES-cents today dislike their work. Assignment to a middle grade school is, all too frequently, the last choice of teachers who are prepared for elementary and secondary education. Teachers view duty in the middle grades as a way station. After suffering through a few years with young adolescents, teachers move on to assignments they prefer and for which they feel they were prepared in their own education.

Other teachers of young adolescents lack confidence in their ability to teach these students.[60] For some, this feeling comes from the structure of middle grade schools; like the students, they feel overwhelmed by the impersonality of the environment, and they feel ineffective with the large number of students they must teach. For others, it comes from a lack of training related to early adolescence, coupled with the pervasive stereotype regarding the near impossibility of teaching young adolescents.

This situation must change drastically. The success of the transformed middle grade school will stand or fall on the willingness of teachers and other staff to invest their efforts in the young adolescent students. Teachers must understand and want to teach young adolescents and find the middle grade school a rewarding place to work.

The Task Force recommends that middle grade education be transformed by:

▲ Developing expert teachers of young adolescents.

DRAMATIC CHANGES ARE NEEDED IN both what individuals learn to become middle grade teachers and how they learn it. Above all else, prospective middle grade teachers need to understand adolescent development through courses and direct experience in middle grade schools. Because they will increasingly be teaching young adolescents of diverse racial and ethnic backgrounds, teachers must also learn about and become sensitive to cultural differences.

Teachers should learn to work as members of a team and, within the team framework, to design and help teach interdisciplinary, developmentally appropriate programs of study. As members of a team, teachers will be responsible for educating other teachers about the importance of key principles, concepts, and facts within their discipline, and for working with colleagues to find common ground in the subjects that they teach.

Teachers in a restructured middle grade school will need education in principles of guidance to serve as advisors. Teachers will also need preparation in working with one- and two-parent families, families of various ethnic and racial backgrounds, and families who for economic or other reasons are undergoing stress that may influence their children's performance in school.

The Task Force envisions one approach to teacher education wherein selection and preparation of expert middle grade teachers begins with undergraduate work, which does not differ from that required for many other professions. Indeed, the bachelor's degree should qualify prospective teachers for many career choices and not lock them into teaching if they decide on an alternative or prove unsuited for the classroom. For those undergraduates who are interested in a teaching career, however, opportunities to observe students in schools and other community settings, and to interact with young adolescents should be available as early as the freshman year.

Undergraduate education should, nevertheless, provide prospective middle grade teachers with a solid core of knowledge in one or more subject areas. Potential middle grade teachers would as undergraduates be expected to concentrate, therefore, on one and preferably two academic subjects such as English, history, mathematics, or biology.

Paid internships or apprenticeships in middle grade schools would follow undergraduate education. Apprentice teachers would teach no more than half-time under continuing guidance from mentor teachers. Mentors drawn from both university faculties and the middle grade school would help student teachers to develop their capacity to work effectively with young adolescents and to make informed decisions about their commitment to a future of teaching young adolescents. (Initially, the pool of mentors will be relatively small, but will increase as education of teachers for the middle grades improves and the number of expert middle grade teachers, from which mentors can be drawn, grows.) While teaching, interns would take graduate courses to further their understanding of young adolescents and the art of teaching as well as their understanding of what is known about the processes of learning.

Selection of teachers to move beyond apprenticeship would be determined largely by their performance in classrooms. Traditional pencil-and-paper tests, which often bear little relation to actual classroom effectiveness, would be replaced with observation of candidates in actual and simulated classrooms and evaluation of candidates' portfolios. Assessments of teachers by mentor teachers and other qualified individuals will screen out candidates who might be more effective in elementary or high school or those who should not enter the teaching profession at all.

Those candidates who are selected move from apprentice to licensed teacher. These teachers would continue graduate coursework aimed at obtaining a master's degree or recertification according to state requirements.

The matter of licensure or certification presents an opportunity to increase the numbers and strengthen the quality of middle grade teachers consonant with procedures currently in place. Teachers are usually licensed and certified (different states use different terms) for either elementary or secondary school, and 23 states offer an additional endorsement or credential for teaching in the middle grades.[61] The Task Force believes that all teachers who are licensed or certified to teach in either elementary or secondary levels should, upon completion of their education in middle grade schools, receive a supplemental endorsement to teach at that level. This endorsement would not prevent them from teaching in elementary or high schools at some other time, if they chose to do so.

A middle grade endorsement could be valuable for three reasons. First, it would recognize the special talents and training of a teacher who has decided to teach young adolescents. Second, it would encourage schools of education to offer specialized courses for the middle grades. Third, it would provide a fully legitimate status for middle grade teachers, something many do not have at this time; prospective teachers are unlikely to prepare for a career for which there is no recognition to practice.

When voluntary certification at standards beyond required state licensure becomes available through the National Board for Professional Teaching Standards in 1993, certification as a teacher with a middle grade specialty is desirable. Such a certification will bring prestige to the job, increase the options for employment, help create a cadre of highly qualified teachers who specialize in young adolescents, and enlarge the pool of professionals qualified to act as team leaders and mentors.

IMPROVING ACADEMIC PERFORMANCE THROUGH BETTER HEALTH AND FITNESS

IT HAS BEEN TAKEN FOR GRANTED that education in this country should emphasize academics over broader concerns for the whole student. Physical and mental health dimensions of educating the young adolescent, dimensions so vital to the ancient Greeks, are largely lost on us Americans. Many schools count on the school nurse to bring some health care to their students, but, with the exception of athletes, many students do not receive the health services they need. In the view of 70 percent of all U.S. teachers, poor health and undernourishment are problems for their students.[62]

School systems are not responsible for meeting every need of their students. But where the need directly affects learning, the school must meet the challenge. So it is with health.

Given a choice, teachers prefer to educate bright, interested, and attentive students. However, teachers find that many of their students are inattentive and disengaged from the learning process. Although good health does not guarantee that students will be interested in learning, ample evidence suggests that the absence of good health lowers students' academic performance. The most obvious example is absences. When health problems cause excessive school absences, students fail to master critical knowledge; once behind in school work, they find it harder and harder to catch up.

Drug and alcohol use increasingly begins in the middle grades. Youth who turn to these substances need immediate access to professional counseling and treatment. Young adolescents are also going through puberty. In addition to clear and accurate instruction in the middle grade curriculum about physical maturation and reproduction, young adolescents often require expert counseling, as well as health services, to help them deal with their emerging sexuality.[63]

Mild to severe mental health problems are widespread among young adolescents, yet they, like all young people in our country, often do not receive the services they need. Nationally, from 12 to 15 percent of all youth (7.5 million to 9.5 million) suffer from emotional or other disorders that warrant mental health treatment. Yet 70 to 80 percent of all youth in need may not receive any mental health services or may receive inappropriate services.[64]

Because of the direct link between the health of young adolescents and their success in school, the Task Force concludes that middle grade schools must accept a significant responsibility, and be provided sufficient resources, to ensure that needed health services are accessible to young adolescents and that schools become health-promoting environments. Schools need not deliver the services directly, but should make sure they are provided. Moreover, the school's role will vary with the availability of family and community resources and with community values. It is essential, however, that every middle grade school have a coordinated system to identify health problems and provide treatment or referral to outside health agencies and individuals.

The transformed middle grade school can meet these objectives by:
▲ Ensuring student access to health services; and
▲ Establishing the school as a health-promoting environment.

IN MANY SCHOOLS TODAY, A SCHOOL
nurse is available to students perhaps once or twice a month. The nurse
necessarily concentrates on students needing immediate attention, which
leaves little time to identify less obvious conditions that might warrant
health care or counseling.

This situation is inadequate and unacceptable. Every middle grade
school should have a school health coordinator whose principal task is to
marshal available health care resources on behalf of students. In many
school districts, the health coordinator might also be a school nurse.
Nurse practitioners are also appropriate candidates. In sparsely popu-
lated districts, one health coordinator might serve several small schools.

The school health coordinator would provide limited medical screening and first aid; refer students to health service practitioners and
agencies outside the school and keep up-to-date records of services
available within the community; follow up on student referrals and assist
students in learning where and how to obtain services; and help to
coordinate health education in school and health-related activities.

School health coordinators should work closely with other support
staff, including guidance counselors, psychologists, food service personnel, and maintenance engineers. Reflecting the spirit of collaboration that
pervades the restructured middle grade school, support staff could be
effectively organized as an advisory team to the principal and to the
school-wide governance committee. The team could coordinate interac-
tions with community health and social service agencies, assist the
principal and the governance committee in establishing health-related
policies in the school, and design and promote health-enhancing
activities. The team could also develop measures aimed at protecting the
confidentiality of students' medical records. The health advisory team
could include student members, who would be actively engaged in
decisions concerning their own well-being and that of their classmates.

In every middle grade school the health and mental health needs of
some students will exceed the immediate resources of school health
personnel. To meet these needs, schools should consider options such as
school-based health clinics (located on school grounds), school-linked
health centers (located off school grounds but joined functionally to the
school and perhaps to other area schools), ties to community health
centers, and arrangements with adolescent services in hospitals or health
maintenance organizations (which might serve both adolescents in school
and those who have dropped out).

School-based health clinics and school-linked health centers have
emerged as extremely promising approaches to ensuring student access
to health and counseling services.[65] Their advantages include convenience
for students, ease in providing follow-up care, fewer potential problems in
cooperating with the school system, increased opportunities for classroom integration of health education activities, and the potential for
increased contact between health clinic or center and classroom personnel. School-based or school-linked clinics also offer the opportunity of
addressing health problems among specific populations of adolescents.
For example, obesity and hypertension, two problems common among the

SCHOOL-BASED HEALTH CARE FOR YOUNG ADOLESCENTS: TRUST IS ESSENTIAL

Although most school-based clinics are located in high schools, educators and health care professionals are increasingly recognizing the need to provide access to health services, especially preventive care and counseling, to young adolescents. Currently, 15 of the approximately 120 school-based clinics in the United States are in middle or junior high schools.

The staff of school-based clinics develop trusting relationships that enable them to address the concerns of young adolescents about their physical and emotional changes. Further, accessibility of the clinics within schools encourages students to seek health care and advice that they might otherwise never experience. Middle grade students are at an age when they might still depend upon parents to take them to health services. The clinics can also help teachers and administrators to understand the developmental needs of their students.

It took a long time to build up the necessary trust, but two school-based clinics sponsored by the Center for Population and Family Health at Columbia University were able to do so and thus to affirm the importance of their services in middle schools. Most of the problems faced by students in the low-income, largely minority schools where the clinics are located are psychosocial, explains Lorraine Tiezzi, director of the project. Consequently, the clinic staff often can reach out to students more effectively than can teachers. "They are not authority figures," she says, "and are perceived by the kids as people who are truly concerned about their personal problems." The clinic staff is also visible in the school building, talking to students in the hallways and cafeteria.

An important factor in building up trust is respect for the privacy of students. The clinic staff members make it clear from the very beginning that any information shared with them will not be shared with other adults, unless it indicates a student may take an action harmful to himself or herself, and even then, the student is informed first.

The clinic staffs are lean: one health services provider, who performs physical examinations and screening, treats minor illnesses, and provides first aid; a health advocate, who works with families and follows through on referrals for students; and a social worker. Graduate students in social work supplement the clinic staff. Students are referred to hospital-based clinic services when needed, such as for contraceptives.

Parent support for the clinics has been strong. Initially, more than 75 percent of parents signed consent forms in one school and 67 percent in the other, with the percentages increasing each of the three years the clinics have been operating, according to Tiezzi.

One clinic has been accepted more by the teaching and administrative staff than the other because the principal has come to see the advantages for his students and teachers, she says. The clinic staff in this school is now providing health education in the classrooms. This is a breakthrough because the Columbia University programs found that educators tend to downplay the importance of adolescent physical development on classroom and personal behavior.

Experience suggests that those who want to provide school clinics must start small — Tiezzi recommends only one school at a time — and with sufficient funds to provide comprehensive services. It takes time to become established and trusted, but the rewards are great.

Black population generally, are often manifest by early adolescence.

Evaluations of school-based clinics, primarily in high schools, indicate that adolescents use them extensively and that parents generally support them. Where school-based clinics are offered, an average of 71 percent of the students enroll. Of those who enroll, a smaller number actually use the centers, ranging from 32 percent to nearly 50 percent. Given that not all students require health or counseling services, these rates of usage are high. Many adolescents who are seen in the health clinics are self-referred, and would not receive health care if the center did not exist.[66]

Most visits to school-linked centers are for physical examinations, acute illnesses, and minor emergencies. School-based clinics report serious conditions in as many as 25 percent of the adolescents they see.[67] Many centers report high rates of depression, and nearly every site reports a high incidence of sexual abuse.[68]

Currently, reports primarily from high school clinics indicate that reproductive health care accounts for fewer than 25 percent of the services provided. In middle grade schools abstinence and prevention counseling in school-based clinics can be critical in convincing young people to abstain from sexual activity until they are older. Evidence suggests that such abstinence counseling can delay the initiation of sexual activity by several months to one year.[69]

It must be recognized, however, that some young people will become sexually active during the middle grade years, no matter how much counseling they receive. By the age of 16, 29 percent of all boys and 13 percent of all girls have become sexually active.[70] Each year, about 60,000 babies are born to young adolescent girls under 15.[71] Therefore, although it is neither the only nor the primary function, providing family planning information is an appropriate role for school-based clinics serving middle grade students.

ESTABLISHING THE SCHOOL AS A HEALTH-PROMOTING ENVIRONMENT

THE MIDDLE GRADE SCHOOL SHOULD provide a model for healthful lifestyles for both students and adults. Schools should emphasize good nutrition consistent with health education messages presented in the classroom. Students should receive sound and up-to-date information on nutrition and diet. They should be served food that is consistent with that information. Offering adolescents foods they learn are unhealthful sends a conflicting message. Food services should eliminate items that are high in animal fat, salt, or sugar, and should substitute healthful snacks such as fruit and fruit juice for candy and soft drinks. Given their rapid growth, young adolescents need foods containing sufficient calcium and iron. Where appropriate, schools can offer special diets for obese children or those on dietary regimens. Schools can add variety and promote awareness of and appreciation for different foods by offering those from many cultures.

Schools should be smoke-free. Schools should prohibit cigarettes on school grounds, and should ban smoking by anyone on the middle grade school campus. The school should offer programs, preferably onsite, to school personnel, students, families, and community members who wish to quit smoking. Not only would this service be convenient, but it would also show everyone in the community that the school considers their health important and takes seriously its health responsibilities to them as well as to their children.

Physical fitness should be a matter of pride for all in the school community, including teachers, staff, and all students. Regular physical education and involvement in sports and fitness activities should be available for students and staff. Under no circumstances should opportunities for regular physical exercise and athletic competition in sports be limited to interscholastic sports. Interscholastic competitive sports may be desirable as a way to recognize young people for excellence, but

VIOLENCE AND CRIME IN SCHOOLS SPUR NEW APPROACHES

Violence and other crime in and near schools has become a matter of serious concern for administrators, teachers, students, and parents. Where petty theft from lockers and occasional fights were once problems, today assaults, carrying of weapons, drug transactions, and robberies are constant worries in many schools.

The amount of school violence and crime is not easily measured, and media accounts of episodes may not accurately reflect crime trends. In any event, the U.S. Department of Justice National Crime Survey indicates that teenagers are victims of crime more frequently than any other age group and that a quarter of crimes committed against them take place in or near schools.

States such as South Carolina have formed task forces to study methods of reducing crime and protecting students. Many school systems have sought professional advice from police and the security industry, hired security directors on staff, and acted to improve physical security of schools.

The notion that violence is preventable underlies the Violence Prevention Project in Boston, which has produced a high school curriculum that has been adapted for middle grade students. The program is targeted at all students. It teaches students to think critically about violence by examining violence in society, on television, and in association with alcohol. Students discuss the costs of violence to both society and the individual and learn methods of conflict resolution by role-playing a variety of conflict situations. By videotaping these encounters, students have opportunities to reflect on their behavior and emotions, and to discuss options for safely resolving conflicts. The curriculum is being tested in Detroit; Philadelphia; Houston; Compton, California; and Gary, Indiana.

The Conflict Resolution Program in San Francisco is aimed at boosting self-esteem and making students more responsible for improving the school's social environment, both of which are factors that program designers see

as vital to retaining truants and potential dropouts. Students learn means of peaceful expression and conflict resolution to settle everyday disputes and to avert violence within crowded urban schools.

In 15 middle grade and high schools in San Francisco, disputes are resolved in a designated room. Students in conflict have the choice of going before two peer conflict managers or an adult. Student conflict managers are nominated by other students, receive 16 hours of training from their teachers (who have in turn been trained by Conflict Resolution Program staff), and work in pairs so that they can discuss cases and arrive at a balanced and impartial position.

In these programs, the energy that might be expended in violence is channeled into creative learning experiences, and the conflicts that might have taken place give way to teamwork and responsible conduct.

physical education should not become a sorting program that focuses only on the most talented. Fitness is a key ingredient of good physical and mental health, which is a critical goal of the core instructional program for all students. Every student should achieve at least moderate success at some type of physical activity, which means that schools must join with parks and recreation departments to offer an array of athletic opportunities.

Above all, schools must be safe places. The changes in middle grade schools suggested in this report, by creating an ethos of mutual support and responsibility, should greatly reduce the conflicts and tensions among youth that lead to violence. Moreover, young people have shown remarkable ability at conflict management and for mediating and resolving conflicts among their peers. Schools should explore these highly promising approaches.

Violence in and around schools is a serious social problem that schools cannot solve alone. Greater efforts and more resources must be forthcoming from local governments to ensure that students are safe both in school and on their way to and from school. Earlier in this century, when automobiles posed a threat to students, schools and law enforcement agencies established school crossing guards. The time has come in some communities to create similar safe access lanes to schools that young people and their parents can be assured are well patrolled. Equally serious are the problems of students and outsiders dealing in drugs or carrying weapons in or near schools.

Stopping violence, drug dealing, and carrying of weapons in and around schools is a matter of the utmost urgency in our society. Perhaps the short-term answer is police action and other safeguards that control school grounds and shield students from such dangers. In the longer run, however, fundamental societal change is needed. Crime and violence are associated with concentrations of poverty, illiteracy, poor housing, and limited opportunities. American society today has not committed itself to addressing these serious and well-documented social problems. Until it does, it can expect little in the way of substantial reduction in crime and violence.

REENGAGING FAMILIES IN THE EDUCATION OF YOUNG ADOLESCENTS

Families and middle grade schools must be allied through trust and respect if young adolescents are to succeed in school.

DESPITE THE CLEARLY DOCUMENTED benefits of parental involvement for students' achievement and attitudes toward school, parental involvement of all types declines progressively during the elementary school years. By middle grade school, the home-school connection has been significantly reduced, and in some cases is nonexistent.[72]

The widening gulf between families and schools during the middle grade years reflects many parents' belief that they should increasingly disengage from their young adolescents. In the belief that adolescents should be independent, parents come to view involvement in their child's education as unnecessary. While young adolescents need greater autonomy, however, they neither need nor desire a complete break with parents and other family members.

For their part, many middle grade schools do not encourage, and some actively discourage, parent involvement at school. Particularly in low-income and minority neighborhoods, parents are often considered to be part of the problem of educating young adolescents rather than an important potential educational resource. Many parents in such communities, after assessing their own poor relations with their young adolescent's teachers and recalling their own painful memories of the classroom, become deeply alienated from their young adolescent's school.[73]

Reversing the downward slide in parent involvement and closing the gulf between parents and school staff with mutual trust and respect are crucial for the successful education of adolescents. Middle grade schools can reengage families by:

▲ Offering parents meaningful roles in school governance;

▲ Keeping parents informed; and

▲ Offering families opportunities to support the learning process at home and at school.

IN AN AMERICA OF SMALL TOWNS and close-knit neighborhoods, schools were a natural part of the community, and trust and respect between schools and families came more readily. Schools today need to reach out to offer families meaningful roles in their child's education and in the life of the school. One method of reaching out to parents and involving them in the education of their young adolescents is to ask them to serve on school-wide building governance committees.

The building governance committee affords parents a meaningful opportunity to help define the mission of the school and to join in the decisionmaking process concerning building-wide issues and problems. The role of parents in defining building-level goals and supporting the school's overall program must be carefully defined and complement rather than conflict with school staff's role in developing the academic program. Yet no middle grade school can successfully serve youth and the community if families do not agree with the school's goals and reinforce them at home.

Parents involved in planning the work of the school feel powerful, develop confidence, and are more likely to attend school activities, which signals the importance of school to their young adolescents. Parents on school-wide governance committees who work effectively and cooperatively with school staff become models of such behavior for their young adolescents and other students.[74]

It is important for young adolescents to see their parents as effective people and as decisionmakers, as people who are concerned about them and who work and act on their behalf. The only place where many young people, particularly in low-income communities, see their parents in important roles is in the school or the church. Even if students do not see their own parents in meaningful roles in school, they benefit from seeing parents of other children in those roles. Parental involvement also has the potential to create trust and respect between parents and school staff; as students observe that trust, they begin to trust school staff as well.[75]

Parent-Teacher Organizations with genuine responsibility for elements of the school program represent another important way in which schools can reach out to involve parents. These organizations can be particularly important in offering parents opportunities to decide what they need to know about early adolescence. In our country, much of parent-adolescent relations involves uncharted waters. Parent-Teacher Associations and Parent-Teacher Organizations can enable parents to find out from others like themselves what "normal" means for this age group. Strong parent organizations can initiate workshops or classes on parenting skills or teach parents how to tutor or monitor their children in specific subjects.

DIRECT COMMUNICATION BETWEEN middle grade schools and parents can be one of the most effective means of establishing trust, and for easing students' transition from elementary to middle grades. Communication between home and school should begin well before the first day of school. To ease the transition, middle grade teachers and administrators can contact parents early and consistently. The traditional open house held several weeks into the youth's first semester comes too late and may attract few parents. Parents need to know how the middle grade school operates, what rules and procedures students should anticipate. Moreover, families need to know before their child enters middle grade school that they are respected and play a central role in the school program.

Schools can promote trust, collaboration, and communication between parents and school staff in other ways. Assigning each student an advisor who meets and comes to know the youth's family over the entire period of enrollment sends a clear signal that the school considers strong linkages with home vital. The advisor should communicate with parents regularly, not only in crises. Advisors should contact parents when something good happens, or ask for help in understanding the youth as an individual. In turn, parents should be encouraged to share their concerns with advisors before problems arise and to make advisors aware of special circumstances that may influence their child's behavior.

Advisors must respect students' privacy. Parents should understand that communications between advisors and students are confidential and that advisors are not free to pass along information they receive from students. In cases where the student is in a truly dangerous situation, the advisor may break this confidentiality, but such cases are rare.

Teachers can forge alliances with parents in planning a course of study during the middle grade years that will enable each young person to reach his or her full potential. Because families and school staff each have separate but interdependent responsibilities in educating the young adolescent, the school should communicate with families as a partner.

One responsibility of parents, for example, would be to participate with their child in conferences with teachers. Conferences of parents, students, and teachers on the student's team to discuss student progress should be held at least once per semester. While it may be impractical for all teachers on a team always to participate, at least two teachers should attend. The independent perspectives of several teachers, offered in the context of a group discussion based on mutual respect, give parents a more complete understanding of how their child is performing. The team conference also reduces the potential for conflicts that can occur with individual teachers, particularly when a teacher comes from a different ethnic, racial, or socioeconomic background.

Consistent positive contact among families, teachers, and advisors helps to create a climate of trust between the primary adult influences on young people's development. In addition, the building governance committee, which includes parent members nominated by parents, serves as an essential mechanism for promoting respectful relations between families and school staff.

PARENTS WHO DO NOT SERVE ON building governance committees or participate in other governance activities can help support the learning process at home or at school. Schools must recognize, however, that significant outreach efforts will be necessary to establish good working relations because many parents sense that they have no meaningful role in their children's education or in the school.

Parents can tutor their young adolescents or monitor completion of homework. Most importantly, they can encourage their children to apply themselves diligently to their schoolwork, maintain good health, and engage in youth service. High expectations can be strongly reinforced at home.

Teachers can design home-learning activities that draw on parents' strengths. For instance, written assignments based on interviews with parents about events that took place during their childhood can bring history alive for the student. Assignments for which young people ask their parents' opinion on current world affairs or issues of the neighborhood can offer students different perspectives on their own studies.

Parents, grandparents, and other adults can also play useful roles in daily school life. Those with particular interests and expertise can serve as classroom resources for presentations and as a source of support materials. They can assist with school clubs and athletics. A parent able to assist in coordinating the school's youth service program represents a significant potential resource.

CONNECTING SCHOOLS WITH COMMUNITIES

Schools and community organizations should share responsibility for each middle grade student's success.

A COMMUNITY THAT SETS OUT TO educate all of its young adolescents to become competent, responsible, and productive adults must marshal its resources behind its schools. In communities with ample or restricted school budgets, resources from the nonprofit and private sectors, health care professions, and other institutions can add intangible and invaluable dimensions to the educational process. No price tag can be placed on the experience that a young adolescent gains, for example, from serving as a volunteer in a home for the elderly.

All communities contain their own human and economic wealth. Finding these resources and linking them in sustained partnerships with schools will be a formidable task. Many schools today have no connection with community organizations. School policies and practices may discourage partnerships with local industry. Schools and businesses or community organizations may have conflicting policies that inhibit cooperation. Concerns about liability and union jurisdiction may pose barriers.

Yet the expense and difficulty of creating partnerships is almost certain to be outweighed by the ensuing benefits. This country's inclination to solve problems at the local level has generated many examples of communities that have reaped such benefits. From a range of such partnerships, the Task Force examines five ways that communities are currently working with middle grade schools by:

▲ Placing students in youth service;

▲ Ensuring student access to health and social services;

▲ Supporting the middle grade education program;

▲ Augmenting resources for teachers and students; and

▲ Expanding career guidance for students.

PLACING STUDENTS IN YOUTH SERVICE

YOUTH SERVICE IN THE COMMUNITY should be part of the core program in middle school education. Students can volunteer to work at senior citizen centers, nursing homes, soup kitchens, child care centers, parks, or environmental centers.

Several national youth organizations consider such service to be an important part of their regular program. Six of these — Boy Scouts, Boys Clubs, Camp Fire, Girls Scouts, Girls Clubs, and 4-H — participate in an annual Youth for America program, sponsored by the Colgate-Palmolive Corporation, that makes awards to local affiliates of these organizations in recognition of exemplary youth service.

The extent to which existing youth-agency service programs are closely integrated into school curricula is unclear, although efforts to do so exist. One good example is the Early Adolescent Helper Program (EAHP) sponsored by The City University of New York. Since its inception in 1982, this program has involved nearly 700 students in 17 New York City middle and junior high schools in structured educational enrichment and youth service. (The school systems of Bridgeport, Connecticut, and Phoenix, Arizona, have adopted this program.)

NEARLY EVERY COMMUNITY HAS A health department, a family planning clinic, or a family counseling agency. Yet to be truly accessible to young adolescents, such services must be well-publicized, affordable, easy to reach, open at appropriate times, and attuned to the needs of adolescents themselves, and they must guarantee confidentiality.

This chapter established earlier that young adolescents must be in good health to learn at school. Following are some specific examples of promising school-community collaborations designed to increase access of young adolescents to needed health and social services.

STUDENT HELPERS FORM COMMUNITY TIES

Connections between the community and the school are one important result of the Early Adolescent Helper Program (EAHP) initiated by The City University of New York. School personnel get to know the people and resources in their community as they seek placements for the Helpers. Community agency staff gain understanding of the schools in their area through what may be their first formal agency contact with the school system. Thus, while the young adolescent Helpers are gaining a sense of belonging to the community, adults in the program are doing the same.

The EAHP trains middle grade students as Helpers and places them in the community for after-school assignments in safe and supervised places. Helpers are sent to child care or Head Start centers, where they read to the children, supervise the playground, assist with the snack, conduct arts and crafts or music

activities, and help with math games. Other Helpers are placed in senior citizen centers, where they join in projects with the elderly, such as interviewing one another on audio or videotape about life experiences of different generations.

An adult, usually a teacher or guidance counselor, trains Helpers in a weekly small-group seminar with hands-on activities designed to build Helpers' skills and prepare them for their role in the community. The seminars emphasize reflection and encourage Helpers to talk about themselves, think about their futures, and take responsibility for their daily lives. Helpers share experiences, ideas, and approaches and discuss their feelings about being a Helper as well as appropriate dress and behavior on their assignments.

Developing trust within the seminar enables Helpers to discuss concerns that are not usually

addressed in school. As young adolescents, for example, they have had little experience in exercising authority or power, and they are able in the seminar to exchange views on this subject.

In one newsletter on the program, Helpers said they learned to listen to others, to trust and be trusted by others, to be patient and reliable, to accept responsibility, and to meet new people who became important to them. They enjoyed getting to know adults at their school outside the usual teacher-student relationships, and especially liked being treated as co-staff, feeling valued for their efforts and opinions, and feeling important to others.

Adults reported in the newsletter that the Helpers acted without exception in a professional manner, attended regularly, and assumed their work roles with complete seriousness. The adults also noted positive attitude and behavior changes.

Community-wide planning is essential to the process of ensuring that adolescents receive the services they need and want. An effort initiated in 1986 by the mayor of Indianapolis and the Community Service Council of Greater Indianapolis, in conjunction with the local United Way, exemplifies good community planning. Principals, teachers, school board members, community leaders, and service providers assess young people's needs, examine current systems for addressing those needs, and recommend changes. This effort is designed to replace a crisis-oriented, problem-specific approach to service delivery with a plan focused on youth development. The plan also establishes a Coordinating Council whose members advise the mayor's office on an ongoing basis and propose more efficient and effective ways of making decisions and allocating resources in all areas affecting services to youth.

New Jersey's School-Based Youth Services Program represents a statewide effort to improve the planning and delivery of comprehensive youth services. Developed by the state Department of Human Services in consultation with the state Department of Education, this program set an ambitious goal: to offer adolescents, especially those experiencing problems, the opportunity to complete their education and acquire the skills necessary for employment or for postsecondary education.

One salient feature of this approach is its clear intent to augment and coordinate — rather than to supplant or duplicate — existing services. A second feature is that while nearly all centers are on school grounds or located within a mile of a school, either schools or community-based organizations, such as local affiliates of the Urban League, can play the lead-agency role in coordinating required services.

SUPPORTING THE MIDDLE GRADE
EDUCATION PROGRAM

MANY LOCAL AGENCIES ASSIST students of all achievement levels, including underachievers. Public libraries provide safe and quiet places to study (a particularly valuable resource in low-income neighborhoods), reference sources, structured programs, and help from qualified professionals.[76] Many youth-serving agencies, particularly the facility-based organizations such as settlement houses, YMCAs and YWCAs, Girls Clubs, and Boys Clubs, offer daily tutoring sessions, homework clinics, and homework hotlines for students. A youth-serving organization in San Diego, California, supplies college students with textbooks so they can respond to teens' hotline requests.

Churches provide social services during after-school hours, either by opening their facilities to students or by providing community service opportunities for students in their congregations. The Congress of National Black Churches launched Project SPIRIT, designed to provide after-school tutoring, homework assistance, and educational enrichment to inner-city youth 6 to 12 years old, and will expand the program to include teenage youth in 1990.

Community agencies support academic goals of schools by offering alternative education services to teenage students who fail or drop out. The Salvation Army, for example, has a long tradition of providing

NEW JERSEY OFFERS SCHOOL-BASED YOUTH SERVICES

Trouble for many young adolescents comes in multiple doses. A young person may have parents who face severe unemployment and housing problems, and a father or mother who is an alcoholic or drug abuser. The young person may be performing poorly at school, lack dental or medical care, and know no reliable adult to whom to turn for advice.

Human service agencies that could help this youth may themselves be geographically dispersed, unattractively labeled or socially unacceptable to young people, and not linked to one another. The agencies may rely heavily on informal referrals, with no systematic intake from the school system, and may, by failing to provide family counseling, be unable or unwilling to address problems in family relationships.

Under the leadership of Governor Thomas H. Kean, New Jersey has established school-based youth service centers that help young people to deal with complex problems they face. The centers also provide counseling to families. The system is based in or linked to schools because, state officials have found, schools offer the most effective sites for reaching and treating large numbers of adolescents on a regular basis.

Communities receiving state funds have the endorsement of the local school district and board of education. The school or organization operating the center targets services to families that have multiple problems and are at risk of becoming dependent on public assistance. Centers try to be sensitive to cultural and linguistic characteristics of the population, for example, through use of Spanish-speaking staff, special efforts to reach Hispanic students who have dropped out, and liaison with cultural groups in the community. They conduct activities, such as special vocational education and recreation, that attract adolescents to the site.

Centers serve young people during and after school hours and during the summer if possible, and involve them in planning and implementation. Centers have an advisory board that includes representatives of service organizations, the New Jersey Education Association, parents of students enrolled in the school, students enrolled in the school who are recommended by the student government, and the family court system. The state also recommends including the school nurse and guidance counselor.

Centers offer adolescents basic services (training or employment services, health screening and referrals, and mental health or family counseling) at a single site. Beyond this core, the state encourages centers to provide child care, parenting skills instruction, and outreach to adolescents who have left school. Although many centers (65 percent) offer family planning, they may not use state funds for that purpose. Others offer child care (44 percent), transportation (62 percent), and a 24-hour hotline (44 percent).

Sites include 25 high schools and 5 vocational schools. Ten of these centers send representatives to local middle grade schools to explain the program to the students and make referrals. Coordinating agencies include schools, nonprofit agencies, mental health agencies, a county health department, a city human resources department, a Private Industry Council, an Urban League, and a community development organization.

The centers serve anyone from 13 to 19 years of age, and have served young people older than 19 who are still in school. Between April and December 1988, the centers served 10,533 individual adolescents and provided some 35,177 services, including multiple services to the same person, repeat visits, and follow-ups. More than half of those services were provided in the core areas of the program: mental health services (35 percent), health (26 percent), and vocational training or other employment (17 percent).

Administratively, the state requires that each host community provide at least 25 percent of program costs through direct financial contribution or inkind services, facilities, or materials. The state pays about $200,000 to each community annually, on average. Stable funding has proven to be a factor in convincing community organizations and schools that they should work together on the program, according to state officials.

alternative education for pregnant teens through its national network of Booth Services. The Boys and Girls Club of Greater Milwaukee collaborates with that city's public school system to sponsor an alternative education program at two club facilities. Both are for middle school students expelled for weapon possession or other unacceptable behavior. Program staff work closely with teachers and administrators in the public schools. They use the school system's basic skills curriculum and supplement it with offerings such as microcomputer training.

Finally, countless community groups, adult sororities and fraternities, and professional and civic groups — such as Kiwanis Clubs, Rotary Clubs, Lions Clubs, the Knights of Columbus, the Junior League, Business and Professional Women, and the American Association of University Women — sponsor annual scholarship competitions and other incentives designed to promote academic achievement.

In addition to supporting students directly, as the preceding examples demonstrate, community organizations can supplement or enhance middle school education. Although enrichment can take place during school hours and on campus, it is more likely to be offered after school, on weekends or during holidays and vacations, and in several non-school settings. For example, science, art, and children's museums have in recent years attracted youth participation by organizing sleepovers and other special events, offering internships, and mounting youth-oriented exhibits. The Association of Science-Technology Centers currently operates a national Community Group Partnership Program that provides minigrants for collaborative projects linking its affiliates with community-based organizations and schools.

Youth agencies have a strong record in educational enrichment. Traditional Scout, Camp Fire, and 4-H programs include weekly sessions, often in school buildings, with volunteer leaders who introduce small groups of young people to activities and subject areas. The young adolescents who participate in these programs are given greater autonomy than their younger counterparts to select topics and activities for their meetings.

Although youth-serving agencies are often perceived as focusing only on such traditional areas as nature appreciation, domestic skills, and community service, in reality all of these groups regularly update their national programs to meet the changing needs of young people. For example, Camp Fire (now a coeducational organization) sponsors a national peace education program; and Girl Scouts of the U.S.A. recently conducted a national leadership training program for adolescent girls.

Another trend among youth agencies is to fill gaps in the regular school curriculum. When Girls Clubs of America concluded that mathematics and science represented a critical filter that prevented young women from gaining equal access to career opportunities, the agency developed a national program called Operation SMART to encourage girls to enroll in science and mathematics courses in school and to consider careers in science and technology.

Women win Nobel prizes in physics, fly as astronauts, and fill most kinds of jobs in the contemporary high-technology workplace. Yet the myth persists, and is widely accepted by many young adolescents, that science and technology are not subjects for girls. Consequently, girls and young women, especially those from low- or middle-income families and from minority families, lack experience and self-confidence in these areas.

An out-of-school program of Girls Clubs of America aims to correct that mistaken view and to direct young adolescents toward science and mathematics as rewarding subjects for study in middle grade school and beyond. Girls Clubs of America serves 250,000 girls and young women, more than two-thirds of whom are from low-income families and about half of whom are members of racial minority groups.

Operation SMART (Science, Mathematics, and Relevant Technology) encourages girls to feel confident about and enjoy science and mathematics. Research shows that girls learn most quickly from hands-on experience, which is ordinarily limited during in-school instruction. Girls also learn best in groups, but again, schools tend to teach individually. Finally, girls confronting science and mathematics in school may feel constrained by the rigid time periods of the daily regimen.

Operation SMART augments in-school instruction by providing exactly these opportunities: hands-on experience, collaboration, and open-ended sessions. Girls Clubs of America found that simple access to mathematics and science activities was not enough. Limiting stereotypes and socially expected behaviors had to be confronted if girls were to overcome their apprehension about science and mathematics and to make up for their lack of experience with machines, science equipment, and technology. Thus, in Operation SMART girls take apart computers, repair bicycles, design electrical circuits, and study buoyancy and gravity during a swim. They learn firsthand about how large machines, such as backhoes, work, and they learn to use heavy power tools as well as screwdrivers and wrenches. They use microscopes and hand lenses, go to an observatory to use a telescope, and then build their own telescopes back at the Club.

Most important, they learn to question and to become skeptical, critical thinkers. Through field trips and counseling, the program ties Operation SMART activities to school work by encouraging girls to take the sequential science courses and higher level mathematics courses that are prerequisites for most college majors and careers in the sciences.

Operation SMART program serves girls from 6 to 18 years old, and is now focusing on the crucial middle grade school ages of 9 to 14. With government, corporate, and private foundation support, the program has developed exercises, materials, and other resources that are used by more than 200 Girls Clubs throughout the country.

Some Operation SMART projects meet on school sites. Girls Club staff often work with school officials to plan programs. In Holyoke, Massachusetts, which has a large Puerto Rican population, Girls Clubs and the school district jointly sponsored, planned, and conducted a bilingual Operation SMART conference called Expanding Your Horizons. Schools released students to attend the event, which attracted more than 100 Puerto Rican girls to talk with Hispanic women whose careers involve science and mathematics.

Operation SMART links schools and Girls Clubs in more than 100 communities across the nation in the shared enterprise of educating young adolescent girls. Operation SMART does not substitute for the education that girls receive in schools. Rather, it supports that education and addresses some of the documented problems in formal education.

AMERICAN BUSINESS SUPPORTS community educational and human services, and recent experience suggests that this support is expanding. Business has both an important civic duty to support public education and good business reasons to do so. Many business leaders see their stake as consisting of a steady flow of qualified workers, a working populace that buys goods and services, and community goodwill that supports business.

Businesses and the professions support local education in two ways. First, they contribute to local nonprofit service agencies that in turn serve students. Second, they enter into partnerships with school systems and contribute funds, equipment, employee time, or other resources. The U.S. Department of Education estimates that American business sponsored some 60,000 school-support projects in 1986.[77] Contributions ranged from gifts of equipment, supplies, and cash to allowing employees salaried leave for counseling, tutoring, or mentoring students.

Examples of business support for elementary and secondary public education abound. Hundreds of schools have received free microcomputers from Apple, International Business Machines Corporation, and other companies. General Electric employees assist science, mathematics, and career development programs through a professional group known as the Elfun Society. Other companies have given funds and equipment to renovate school buildings, convert them to uses such as a science center, and established an endowment to pay for operating costs.

Some observers have cautioned that certain kinds of business support may bring with it influences that educators, parents, and students may find objectionable or at least troublesome. A business supporter might want to advertise its product to students, for example, or otherwise influence school authorities or students in the direction of purchasing its products or services.

Finally, it is important to remember that the most significant contribution of business is not direct support to middle grade schools. It is support of adequate and equitable financing of the public schools and an insistence that the schools produce students who are properly prepared for the workforce and who are good citizens.

Universities are another resource that can directly enrich a middle grade school's curriculum or support the educational program in other ways. Claremont Middle School in Oakland, California, for example, has tapped the creativity and energy of the University of California at Berkeley to enrich its curriculum. Scientists from the Lawrence Livermore National Laboratory, a world-famous center for nuclear physics research associated with the university, help 6th and 7th grade students on projects, organize field trips, and assist in the school's computer program, which is a magnet for middle school students in the Oakland system.

In the Intergenerational Science Program, senior citizens, some of whom have had careers in science, are trained at Lawrence Hall of Science, an institution dedicated to education and associated with the university, to go into 8th grade life sciences classes. Accompanied by

Lawrence Hall staff and using Lawrence Hall materials, animals, or interactive equipment, the seniors present science projects to the students.

THE GUIDANCE PROGRAM IN MANY middle schools helps students to select academic courses in the context of career plans. Unfortunately, most schools do little to help students to learn about career or employment options. Recent surveys indicate that young people desire more information about career planning and that school counselors are responsible for far too many students to provide individualized career counseling.[78]

In many communities, urban as well as rural, agencies such as Junior Achievement, Future Homemakers of America, and Future Farmers of America offer in-school and out-of-school career guidance and skill-building. In recent years, other youth agencies have joined this effort. For example, Boy Scouts of America's fastest growing program is its Career Explorers, a school-linked career awareness program for adolescent boys and girls initiated in 1983. Nearly 700,000 adolescents participated in this program during 1987. When the program is launched at a particular school, organizers conduct a career-interest survey of all students there. School-based seminars and assemblies address these interests and students are invited to participate in out-of-school career exploration sessions. Guided by an adult mentor, students of like interests form small groups to study their choices and often to talk with local business persons and other adults.

Professional organizations can also help. The Business and Professional Women's Association, for example, sponsors a 10-state career development program that links its members with groups of teenage girls in local communities. In most programs, adult-teenage linkages occur through collaboration with the schools, with community-based youth agencies, or with all groups working together.

Business-sponsored career development initiatives represent a third form of guidance. Some of these efforts match young adolescents with adult employees and workplaces. The programs most suited to the needs and interests of this age group, however, allow young people to explore a wide range of options and work settings.

BUILDING A FUTURE FOR YOUNG ADOLESCENTS IN AMERICA

Neglected as it may be in policymaking, middle grade education is nonetheless generating intense interest in many state and local school systems. In scattered but impressive experiments, some of which are noted in this report, schools and communities are combining resources to change fundamentally their approach to teaching young adolescents.

But change in a few states and communities does not make a national movement. All states and communities must join in this effort.

The Task Force presents in this chapter starting points for transforming middle grade education to meet the needs of our society in the 21st century. The Task Force calls on everyone concerned about young adolescents — leaders in education, health, youth-serving and community organizations, state and federal government, the private sector, and philanthropy as well as parents — to join in this effort. The Task Force calls on all of these sectors to raise public awareness about the need for basic reform and to create the political pressure that will make change a reality.

EDUCATORS

PREPARING ALL YOUTH FOR THE demands of the 21st century requires a redefinition of middle grade education. In keeping with the American tradition of local responsibility for public elementary and secondary education, the Task Force proposes a genuine partnership among teachers, principals, superintendents, local school boards, and community organizations.

Fundamental restructuring in existing educational policies and practices must occur. School boards and superintendents must find ways to authorize and enable principals and teachers to experiment in redefining the mission of middle grade schools and changing current practices. Appropriate measures of student performance that reflect the goals of the transformed middle grade school must be developed to evaluate new approaches.

Colleges and universities can assume important roles. Significant changes are required in the preparation of teachers. Schools of education are one focal point for bringing about these changes. Some schools of education and departments within institutions of higher learning, for example, already collaborate with local school systems to work with middle grade school principals and teachers as they begin the transformation process. Other ways to collaborate might include programs for staff development, mentoring, or tutoring that can help middle grade school administrators, teachers, and students.

Universities, colleges, and schools can also join in programs that provide middle grade schools with apprenticeship opportunities in a variety of fields at the university. Such collaborative experiences could be especially helpful in easing the difficulties that many minority students face when they later make the transition to colleges and universities with predominantly White enrollment.

ACCESS TO HEALTH SERVICES AND instruction in how to maintain good health are essential to the education of young adolescents. Health professionals are encouraged to work and build cooperative relationships with the education sector to promote and support the healthy development of young adolescents.

Health professionals are critical in helping to reshape the school as a health-promoting environment. They can support the core academic programs that teach knowledge of human biology, which assist young people in avoiding health-damaging behaviors. They are needed as advocates in forming school policies on nutrition, smoking, injury prevention, and health and fitness of school staff. They can contribute to local health awareness campaigns in the media, and ensure that messages about health practices that appear in stores, restaurants, convenience markets, parks, and other sites in the community are consistent with what students learn in school. They can develop public information campaigns to raise awareness of the critical health risks that young adolescents face and the need for public support of health care for those young people. These mutually reinforcing layers of positive health messages have proven to be effective in several community-based health promotion efforts.[79]

YOUTH-SERVING AND OTHER COM- munity organizations represent a rich potential source for extending the educational experiences of young adolescents outside the classroom. With their long history of working with youth, these groups are natural members of collaborative efforts with educators and health professionals to transform middle grade schools. Working with schools, youth-serving agencies can become partners in a broader system of youth development, and can assume responsibility for key elements of a transformed school program. These agencies and organizations can develop programs aimed specifically at attracting young people from middle grade schools after school, on weekends, and during the summer, when young adolescents are full of energy and may be most vulnerable to the negative pressures of peers or to undesirable adult influences.

INCREASINGLY, OUR NATION HAS turned to state governments to lead the effort to change America's schools. States can be most constructive by building consensus in and strengthening the capacity of local communities to transform schools. In some states, the superintendent of education may be the appropriate official to lead this effort; in others, the governor may assume that role.

States can immediately convene task forces to review the recommendations in this report and determine what must occur to enable their adaptation to the needs and circumstances of local communities. The task forces should represent all sectors, including state and local government, the education and health systems, the youth-serving sector, parents, business, and community organizations.

States can marshal resources to develop incentives for school districts to transform their middle grade schools and to remove obstacles standing in the way of reform. They can offer a significant reduction in regulations that do not impair safety, health, or civil rights of students, and in return should expect schools to be accountable for student performance.

States can also encourage collaboration at the local level among schools, health and social service agencies, and youth-serving organizations. Specifically, states can devise funding mechanisms that provide new financial incentives or reallocate existing funds to encourage and support collaborative ventures. States should also ensure the equitable distribution of resources among school districts.

FEDERAL LEADERSHIP

THE EDUCATION AND HEALTH OF America's youth are national concerns requiring national leadership. The Task Force urges the President to take the lead in fostering broad-based national recognition of the risks and opportunities that young adolescents face.

In a technology-based economy, the federal government must increasingly support mathematics and science education at all levels. That support might include research and demonstration, technical assistance, dissemination, and other support to assist states and localities in efforts to transform middle grade schools. Also, as current teachers retire, the need for large-scale preparation of teachers who are expert in educating young adolescents will rapidly increase and may well require federal support.

The federal government can also examine its appropriate role in assisting states and localities to come to grips with the problems and the opportunities of early adolescence. The federal government can play a supportive role in the efforts of state and local education, health, and human service departments to undertake pilot testing of the recommendations in this report. The U.S. Department of Education and other relevant agencies should agree to waive nonessential regulations that inhibit such experimentation.

Congress can consider the implications of this report for the rethinking of youth policy at the national level. Many federal agencies, including the Departments of Defense, Health and Human Services (HHS), Justice, and Labor, now support education and training of adolescents. Congress should review these efforts in light of the recommendations of this report. Given the fundamental link between education and health, HHS should pay special attention to opportunities to support research and demonstrations that help young adolescents to adopt healthful lifestyles. Such an effort would likely result in significant savings in long-term health care costs and in increased workplace productivity.

In particular, Congress should examine the assertion in this report

▲ *Determine whether technical assistance is available to divide large schools into several sub-schools or houses and to create teams.* Are schools organized to recognize the needs of students aged 10 to 15 for stable and supportive relationships with peers and teachers? Do teachers have sufficient common planning time to operate effectively as a team?

▲ *Review the core curriculum.* Does the curriculum pay appropriate attention not only to challenging levels of mathematics, science, languages, and social studies, but also to health and community service? Are there opportunities for every student to be recognized for being good at something?

▲ *Examine curriculum frameworks and requirements, and textbook selection procedures.* Does the state emphasize a subject-specific orientation or interdisciplinary, developmentally appropriate curriculum matter? Do students have opportunities to study fundamental principles in depth or is coverage of material emphasized? Does the assessment of student progress reflect the goals of instruction?

▲ *Examine expectation levels for students reflected in test requirements, grade-retention standards, and policies toward between-class ability grouping.* Do the policies result in greater or less student success? Are alternatives to tracking, such as cooperative learning and student tutoring, used? Are opportunities to support students' learning beyond the schoolhouse used?

▲ *Consider school governance standards.* Is there a school-wide mechanism for discussion and decisionmaking involving the entire school community? Do teachers have the authority and resources to design personalized educational experiences for students?

▲ *Evaluate the physical and mental health of the 10- to 15-year-old population.* How prevalent is teenage pregnancy? How extensive is the use of alcohol, drugs, and cigarettes? Are there effective programs of preventive education available to all students? Do students have access to basic health care? Where are the gaps?

▲ *Inventory community resources to identify local organizations and individuals willing to work with schools in a supportive role.* What local youth-serving organizations, voluntary agencies, businesses, and churches are interested in participating in the transformation process? What civic groups and foundations will underwrite collaborative experiments that strengthen education for young adolescents?

▲ *Examine certification standards.* Do the standards require, encourage, or permit special emphasis on the needs of students aged 10 to 15? Do the requirements for recertification or permanent certification include coursework in adolescent development and field experience related to 10- to 15-year-olds?

▲ *Evaluate the nature and character of staff development for experienced teachers.* Is an appropriate orientation available for middle grade school teachers? Is staff development designed to help teachers understand adolescent development and assist them to plan and function as a team?

▲ *Consider incentives that attract teachers to service in middle grade schools.* What incentives would increase interest of teachers in working with young adolescents and making a commitment to middle grade education?

▲ *Assess the role parents are allowed in the middle grade program.* How and when do teachers communicate with parents? Do parents feel welcome in the middle grade buildings? Do parents feel that they have any significant decisionmaking role? Is the school sensitive to demands in the lives of families?

▲ *Assess the morale of teachers and students in the middle grade program.* Do teachers as well as students feel alienated and overwhelmed? Would teachers prefer to teach elsewhere? Do they feel effective as teachers?

that the nation's investment in early education is endangered because so few of those children served in the early stages of their lives will receive the attention they need in middle grade schools. As one example, Chapter I funds reach only about half of eligible children, the vast majority of whom are in elementary schools. Large numbers of eligible students in middle grade schools are never served but could be with increased funding.

THE PRIVATE SECTOR AND PHILANTHROPY

SEVERAL FOUNDATIONS ARE INVOLVED in supporting experimentation in middle grade schools. These and many other efforts around the country will produce an abundance of new ideas and valuable experience. Yet, much of this information could be lost unless mechanisms are devised to share it widely. An ongoing forum is needed to bring together educators, health care professionals, youth-serving organization leaders, business representatives, and government officials to share information among those involved in experimenting in middle grade education and those eager to do so. Such a forum would also examine mechanisms to provide technical assistance to schools and school districts to develop and evaluate their innovations. A forum would create a network of individuals and organizations that can serve as a nucleus for a movement for change in middle grade education.

Businesses and foundations should consider creating and supporting such a forum at the national level and its regional and local equivalents. The federal government and states should be invited to contribute to these efforts.

Private businesses and foundations should also help to create and finance trusts or other philanthropic devices that can support middle grade school innovation. Many of the reforms required in middle grade education may not show immediate results, and they must be insulated from the vicissitudes of annual funding cycles.

PARENTS

PARENTS HAVE AN ENORMOUS STAKE in ensuring the positive outcome of middle grade schools envisioned in this report. Through their alliance with the school, service on governance committees, and support of teachers and of their adolescents, parents can play a key role in the school community itself.

But parents' roles go beyond that. As taxpayers and advocates for adolescents, parents are in a unique position to bring pressure for change in education, health care, and school-community partnerships. Parents, with other taxpayers, support the public schools and are entitled to demand and receive from schools far better performance than schools now deliver.

The energy of parents, in all its manifestations, must be harnessed in the service of advocacy for change within democratic and cooperative avenues. We urge parents to consider the implications of this report and to ensure that their adolescents—and all adolescents—receive the education and health care that they deserve.

EACH OF US IN THIS NATION HAS A stake in fundamentally transforming the educational experiences of young adolescents. In every city, suburb, and rural community, all of us concerned with the development of youth 10 to 15 years old must work together to make the vision in this report a practical reality. This chapter identifies some, although certainly not all, of the starting points to accomplish that goal.

There is, however, another challenge for those already deeply concerned about young adolescents' future and the future of our nation. The crisis our country faces with respect to the preparation of youth for the 21st century is largely unrecognized by the general public. Moreover, some people who would review the current state of affairs with regard to the nation's youth might conclude that no crisis exists at all.

Perhaps the greatest challenge, then, is to make the case to the American public for transforming middle grade schools. A profound change is needed in how Americans view the education of young adolescents, from one that tolerates institutions that regularly fail to prepare millions of young people for productive and fulfilling adult lives, to one that demands of those same institutions success for all young adolescents. In short, a large and activist constituency for changing middle grade schools across the nation must be created if systematic improvement in the education of young adolescents is to occur.

Increasing public awareness and building a national constituency of concern for young people will not be easy, nor will it come quickly. It will require well-planned, collaborative, and sustained efforts, beginning in individual communities and extending to the nation at large. Creating such a constituency by the beginning of the 21st century will itself represent an enormous step forward. Yet it is a step that must be taken if this nation is to avoid becoming a divided society of the affluent and well-educated and the poor and ill-educated.

America's challenge in preparing its youth is truly a formidable task. But many proven and promising solutions exist. We do not lack the knowledge to transform the education of young adolescents. What we need is the leadership and the will.

ENDNOTES

1. Johnston, L. D., O'Malley, P. M., & Bachman, J. G. (1988). *Illicit drug use, smoking and drinking by America's high school students, college students, and young adults: 1975–1987* (DHHS Publication No. (ADM) 89–1602). Washington, DC: U.S. Government Printing Office.

2. Kandel, D. B. (1985). Effects of drug use from adolescence to young adulthood on participation in family and work roles. In R. Jessor (Chair), *Longitudinal research on substance use in adolescence.* Symposium conducted at the meeting of the International Society for the Study of Behavioral Development, Tours, France.

3. Hofferth, S. L., Kahn, J. R., & Baldwin, W. (1987). Premarital sexual activity among U.S. teenage women over the past three decades. *Family Planning Perspectives, 19*(2), 46–53.

4. Hayes, C. D. (Ed.). (1987). *Risking the future: Adolescent sexuality, pregnancy, and childbearing.* Washington, DC: National Academy Press.
   Furstenberg, F. F., Jr., Brooks-Gunn, J., & Morgan, S. P. (1987). *Adolescent mothers in later life.* New York: Cambridge University Press.

5. National Institutes on Allergies and Infectious Disease Study Group. (1980). *Sexually transmitted diseases — Summary and recommendations.* Washington, DC: U.S. Department of Health, Education, and Welfare, National Institutes of Health.

6. *Chartbook on adolescent health.* (in press). Rockville, MD: Public Health Service, Health Resources and Services Administration, Bureau of Health Care Delivery and Assistance, Division of Maternal and Child Health.

7. Waller, A. E., Baker, S. P., & Szocka, A. (1989). Childhood injury deaths: National analysis and geographic variations. *American Journal of Public Health, 79*(3), 310–315.

8. Dusek, J. B. (1987). *Adolescent development and behavior.* Englewood Cliffs, NJ: Prentice-Hall.

9. Dryfoos, J. G. (in press). *Adolescents at risk.* New York: Oxford University Press.

10. Jessor, R. (1984). Adolescent development and behavioral health. In J. D. Matarazzo, S. M. Weiss, J. A. Herd, N. E. Miller, & S. M. Weiss (Eds.), *Behavioral health: A handbook of health enhancement and disease prevention* (pp. 69–90). New York: Wiley.

11. Petersen, A. C. (1988). Adolescent development. *Annual Review of Psychology, 39*, 583–607.

12. Bachman, J. G., Green, S., & Wirtanen, I. D. (1971). Dropping out — problem or symptom. *Youth in Transition, Volume III.* Ann Arbor, MI: Institute for Social Research, University of Michigan.

13. Hirano-Nakanishi, M. (1984). *Hispanic school dropouts: The extent and relevance of pre-high school attrition and delayed education.* Los Alamitos, CA: National Center for Bilingual Research.

14. Jenkins, A. E., III (1988, October). *A study of students who left: D.C. public school dropouts.* Washington, DC: District of Columbia Public Schools, Division of Quality Assurance and Management Planning.

15. Natriello, G., McDill, E. L., & Pallas, A. M. (1987). *In our lifetime: Schooling and the disadvantaged.* Unpublished manuscript.

16. Dryfoos, J. G. (in press). *Adolescents at risk.* New York: Oxford University Press.

17. Lapointe, A. E., Mead, N. A., & Phillips, G. W. (1989, January). *A world of differences: An international assessment of mathematics and science.* Princeton, NJ: Educational Testing Service.

18. National Assessment of Educational Progress. (1985). *The reading report card, progress toward excellence in our schools, trends in reading over four national assessments, 1971–1984.* Princeton, NJ: Educational Testing Service.

19. Applebee, A., Langer, J., & Mullis, I. (1986). *The writing report card, writing achievement in American schools.* Princeton, NJ: National Assessment of Educational Progress, Educational Testing Service.

20. Mark, J. A. (1987, April). Technological change and employment: Some results from BLS research. *Monthly Labor Review, 110,* 26–29.

   Bailey, T. (1988, April). *The new economy, new skills, and the limits of educational reform.* Paper presented at the meeting of the American Educational Research Association, New Orleans, LA.

21. *The forgotten half: Pathways to success for America's youth and young families.* (1988). Washington, DC: Youth and America's Future: The William T. Grant Commission on Work, Family and Citizenship.

22. Ibid.

23. Catterall, J. S. (1987). On the social costs of dropping out of school. *The High School Journal, 71*(1), 19–30.

24. Ibid.

25. U.S. Bureau of the Census. (1987). *Statistical abstract of the United States: 1988* (108th Edition). Washington, DC: U.S. Government Printing Office.

   The forgotten half: Pathways to success for America's youth and young families. (1988). Washington, DC: Youth and America's Future: The William T. Grant Commission on Work, Family and Citizenship.

26. Berlin, G., & Sum, A. (1988). *Toward a more perfect union: Basic skills, poor families, and our economic future* (Occasional Paper Number Three). New York: The Ford Foundation, Project on Social Welfare and the American Future.

27. Center for Population Options. (1988). *Estimates of public costs for teenage childbearing in 1987.* Washington, DC: Author.

28. Institute of Medicine. (1984). *Preventing low birth weight.* Washington, DC: National Academy Press.

   National Commission to Prevent Infant Mortality. (1988). *Death before life: The tragedy of infant mortality.* Washington, DC: Author.

29. Children's Defense Fund. (1988). *Teenage pregnancy: An advocates guide to the numbers.* Washington, DC: Adolescent Pregnancy Prevention Clearinghouse.

30. Harwood, H. J., Napolitano, D. M., Kristiansen, P. L., & Collins, J. J. (1980). *Economic costs to society of alcohol and drug abuse and mental illness: 1980* (Publication No. RTI/2734/00–01FR, June 1984). Research Triangle Park, NC: Research Triangle Institute.

31. Eccles, J. S., & Midgley, C. (in press). Stage/environment fit: Developmentally appropriate classrooms for early adolescents. In R. E. Ames & C. Ames (Eds.), *Research on motivation in education* (Vol. 3). New York: Academic Press.

32. Simmons, R. G., Rosenberg, M., & Rosenberg, F. (1973). Disturbance in the self-image at adolescence. *American Sociological Review, 39*(5), 553–568.

Blyth, D. A., Simmons, R. G., & Carlton-Ford, S. (1983). The adjustment of early adolescents to schools transitions. *Journal of Early Adolescence, 3*(1 & 2), 105–120.

Simmons, R. G., & Blyth, D. A. (1987). *Moving into adolescence: The impact of pubertal change and school context.* Hawthorne, NY: Aldine.

33. Keating, D. P. (1988, July). [Cognitive processes in adolescence] (draft). In G. R. Elliott & S. S. Feldman (Eds.), [*Volume on Normal Adolescent Development*] (in preparation). Stanford, CA: Stanford University and Carnegie Corporation of New York.

34. Arhar, J. M., Johnston, J. H., & Markle, G. C. (1989). The effects of teaming on students. *Middle School Journal, 20*(3), 24–27.

35. Otto, L. B. (1982). *Youth and careers: A parent's guide.* Boys Town, NB: Youth Career Services.

36. Resnick, L. B. (1987). *Education and learning to think.* Washington, DC: National Academy Press.

37. Keating, D. P. (1988, July). [Cognitive processes in adolescence] (draft). In G. R. Elliott & S. S. Feldman (Eds.), [*Volume on Normal Adolescent Development*] (in preparation). Stanford, CA: Stanford University and Carnegie Corporation of New York.

Petersen, A. C. (1983). Pubertal change and cognition. In J. Brooks-Gunn & A. C. Petersen (Eds.), *Girls at puberty: Biological and psychosocial perspective.* New York: Plenum.

Graber, J. A., & Petersen, A. C. (in press). Cognitive changes at adolescence: Biological perspectives. In K. Gibson & A. C. Petersen (Eds.), *The brain and behavioral development: Biosocial dimensions.* New York: Aldine.

38. American Association for the Advancement of Science. (1989). *Science for all Americans: A project 2061 report on literacy goals in science, mathematics, and technology.* Washington, DC: Author.

39. Botvin, G. J., & Wills, T. A. (1985). Personal and social skills training: Cognitive-behavioral approaches to substance abuse prevention. In: C. Bell & R. Battjes (Eds.), *Prevention research: Deterring drug abuse among children and adolescents.* Washington, DC: National Institute on Drug Abuse Research Monograph.

Flay, B. R. (1985). Psychosocial approaches to smoking prevention: A review of findings. *Health Psychology, 4*(5), 449–488.

Flay, B. R. (1985). What do we know about the social influences approach to smoking prevention? Review and recommendations. In: C. Bell & R. Battjes (Eds.), *Prevention research: Deterring drug abuse among children and adolescents.* Washington, DC: National Institute on Drug Abuse Research Monograph.

Glasgow, R. E., & McCaul, K. D. (1985). Life skills training programs for smoking prevention: Critique and directions for future research. In: C. Bell & R. Battjes (Eds.), *Prevention research: Deterring drug abuse among children and adolescents.* Washington, DC: National Institute on Drug Abuse Research Monograph.

40. Botvin, G. J., Baker, E., Botvin, E. M., Filazzola, A. D., & Millman, R. (1984). Alcohol abuse prevention through the development of personal and social competence: A pilot study. *Journal of Studies on Alcohol, 45,* 550–552.

Botvin, G. J., Baker, E., Renick, N., Filazzola, A. D., & Botvin, E. M. (1984). A cognitive-behavioral approach to substance abuse prevention. *Addictive Behaviors, 9,* 137–147.

Botvin, G. J., Baker, E., Filazzola, A. D., Botvin, E. M., Danilo, M., & Dusenbury, L. (1985, August). *A cognitive-behavioral approach into substance abuse prevention: A one year follow-up.* Paper presented at the 93rd annual meeting of the American Psychological Association, Los Angeles.

McAlister, A. L., Perry, C. L., Killen, J., Slinkard, L. A., & Maccoby, N. (1980). Pilot study of smoking, alcohol and drug abuse prevention. *American Journal of Public Health, 70,* 719–721.

41. Schinke, S. P. (1984). Preventing teenage pregnancy. In M. Hensen, R. M. Eisler, & P. M. Miller (Eds.), *Progress in behavior modification* (Vol. 16). New York: Academic Press.

42. Resnick, L. B. (1987). The 1987 presidential address: Learning in school and out. *Educational Researcher, 16*(9), 13–20.

43. Wiggins, G. (1989). Teaching to the (authentic) test. *Educational Leadership, 46*(7), 41–47.

Archibald, D., & Newmann, F. (1988, August). *Beyond standardized testing: Authentic academic achievement in the secondary school.* Reston, VA: National Association of Secondary School Principals.

44. Keating, D. P. (1988, July). [Cognitive processes in adolescence] (draft). In G. R. Elliott & S. S. Feldman (Eds.), [*Volume on Normal Adolescent Development*] (in preparation). Stanford, CA: Stanford University and Carnegie Corporation of New York.

45. Shepard, L. A. (1989). Why we need better assessments. *Educational Leadership, 46*(7), 4–9.

46. Rothman, R. (1988, October 26). Vermont plans to pioneer with "work portfolios." *Education Week, 8*(8), 1.

47. McPartland, J. M., Coldiron, J. R., & Braddock, J. H., II (1987, June). *School structures and classroom practices in elementary, middle, and secondary schools.* Baltimore, MD: The Johns Hopkins University, Center for Research on Elementary and Middle Schools.

48. Oakes, J. (1985). *Keeping track: How schools structure inequality.* New Haven: Yale University Press.

Goodlad, J. I. (1984). *A place called school.* New York: McGraw-Hill.

49. Massachusetts Advocacy Center and the Center for Early Adolescence (1988, July). *Before it's too late: Dropout prevention in the middle grades.* Boston, MA and Carrboro, NC: Authors.

50. Goodlad, J. I. (1984). *A place called school.* New York: McGraw-Hill.

51. Newmann, F. M., & Thompson, J. A. (1987). *Effects of cooperative learning on achievement in secondary schools: A summary of research.* Madison, WI: University of Wisconsin, National Center on Effective Secondary Schools.

Slavin, R. E. (1983). When does cooperative learning increase student achievement? *Psychological Bulletin, 94,* 429–445.

Johnson, D. W., Maruyama, G., Johnson, R., Nelson, D., & Skon, L. (1981). Effects of cooperative competitive, and individualistic goal structures on achievement: A meta-analysis. *Psychological Bulletin, 89,* 47–62.

52. Skon, L., Johnson, D., & Johnson, R. (1981). Cooperative peer interaction versus individual competition and individualistic efforts: Effects on the acquisition of cognitive reasoning strategies. *Journal of Educational Psychology, 73,* 83–92.

53. Slavin, R. E. (1985). Cooperative learning: Applying contact theory in desegregated schools. *Journal of Social Issues, 41*(3), 45–62.

54. Slavin, R. E. (1984). Team assisted individuation: cooperative learning and individualized instruction in the mainstreamed classroom. *Remedial and Special Education, 5*(6), 33–42.

Johnson, D. W., & Johnson, R. T. (1980). Integrating handicapped children into the mainstream. *Exceptional Children, 47,* 90–98.

55. Cohen, P. A., Kulik, J. A., & Kulik, C-L. C. (1982). Educational outcomes of tutoring: A meta-analysis of findings. *American Educational Research Journal, 19*(2), 237–248.

Devin-Sheehan, L., Feldman, R. S., & Allen, V. L. (1976). Research on children tutoring children: A critical review. *Review of Educational Research, 46,* 355–385.

56. Hedin, D. (1986, April). *Students as teachers: A tool for improving school climate and productivity.* Washington, DC: Carnegie Forum on Education and the Economy, a Program of Carnegie Corporation of New York.

57. Epstein, J. L. (1987, January). *Target: An examination of parallel school and family structures that promote student motivation and achievement.* Baltimore, MD: The Johns Hopkins University, Center for Research on Elementary and Middle Schools.

58. Eccles, J. S., & Midgley, C. (in press). Stage/environment fit: Developmentally appropriate classrooms for early adolescents. In R. E. Ames & C. Ames (Eds.), *Research on motivation in education* (Vol. 3). New York: Academic Press.

59. Comer, J. P. (1980). *School power: Implications of an intervention project.* New York: The Free Press.

60. Eccles, J. S., & Midgley, C. (in press). Stage/environment fit: Developmentally appropriate classrooms for early adolescents. In R. E. Ames & C. Ames (Eds.), *Research on motivation in education* (Vol. 3). New York: Academic Press.

61. Children's Defense Fund. (1988). *Survey of state policies and programs in the middle grades.* Washington, DC: Author.

62. The Carnegie Foundation for the Advancement of Teaching. (1988). *The condition of teaching: A state-by-state analysis, 1988.* Princeton, NJ: Princeton University Press.

63. Girls Clubs of America. (1988). *Facts and reflections on girls and substance use.* New York: Author.

64. U.S. Congress, Office of Technology Assessment. (1986, December). *Children's mental health: Problems and services — A background paper.* (OTA Publication No. OTA-BP-H-33). Washington, DC: U.S. Government Printing Office.

65. Millstein, S. G. (August 1988). *The potential of school-linked centers to promote adolescent health and development.* Washington, DC: Carnegie Council on Adolescent Development.

66. Ibid.

67. Ibid.

68. Ibid.

69. Zabin, L. S., Hirsch, M. B., Smith, E. A., Street, R., & Hardy, J. B. (1986). Evaluation of a pregnancy prevention program for urban teenagers. *Family Planning Perspectives, 18,* 119–126.

70. Hayes, C. D. (Ed.). (1987). *Risking the future: Adolescent sexuality, pregnancy, and childbearing.* Washington, DC: National Academy Press.

71. Ibid.

72. Epstein, J. L. (1986). Parents' reactions to teacher practices of parent involvement. *Elementary School Journal, 86,* 277–294.

73. Comer, J. P. (1980). *School power: Implications of an intervention project.* New York: The Free Press.

74. Ibid.

75. Ibid.

76. Weeks, A. C. (1987). There's always something happening at the library. In B. Hatcher (Ed.), *Learning Opportunities Beyond the School,* (pp. 12–17). Wheaton, MD: Association for Childhood Education International.

77. *The forgotten half: Pathways to success for America's youth and young families.* (1988). Washington, DC: Youth and America's Future: The William T. Grant Commission on Work, Family and Citizenship.

78. Otto, L. B. (1982). *Youth and careers: A parent's guide.* Boys Town, NB: Youth Career Services.

79. Perry, C. L. (1984). Health promotion at school: Expanding the potential for prevention. *School Psychology Review, 13*(2), 141–149.

THE EDUCATION AND HEALTH OF **ACKNOWLEDGMENTS**
young adolescents has been a longtime concern of Carnegie Corporation of New York President David A. Hamburg. Stimulated by his leadership, the Board of Trustees established the Carnegie Council on Adolescent Development, which in turn formed the Task Force on Education of Young Adolescents. Dr. Hamburg's clear vision and unflagging commitment to act on the recommendations of the Task Force have been a source of support to all who have worked to prepare this report.

The Task Force deeply appreciates the work of the Chair, David Hornbeck, and Project Director, Anthony Jackson. In addition to his own substantial and insightful contributions, David Hornbeck's diplomatic leadership kept our wide-ranging discussions focused and productive. As the primary author of the report through all its stages, Anthony Jackson successfully synthesized a wide range of knowledge from research and practice, while challenging the Task Force with his own thoughtful conceptions of middle grade education.

We are especially indebted to Vivien Stewart, Chair of Carnegie Corporation's program on Prevention of Damage to Children, and Alden Dunham, Chair of the Corporation's program on Education: Science, Technology, and the Economy. Their strong support of the Task Force's effort and many contributions to the report have proven invaluable.

The views and experience of teachers, administrators, and students in middle schools across the country influenced the content of this report. We are especially grateful to the staff and students at Central Park East Secondary School, New York, NY; Challenger Middle School, Colorado Springs, CO; Charles Eliot Junior High, Cleveland, OH; Jackie Robinson Middle School, New Haven, CT; Louis Armstrong Middle School, Queens, NY; and the Taylor Academy School, University Heights, OH.

Our effort was significantly assisted by the scholarship and advice of many distinguished individuals in the education, health, youth-serving, and policymaking communities. We thank the authors of the commissioned papers for their substantial contributions produced under the most arduous of timetables. Invited participants at the Task Force's meetings and attendees at the four workshops convened by the Task Force provided invaluable guidance. The names of all of these individuals are listed in the appendices.

The Task Force is deeply grateful to the many organizations and leaders who provided opportunities for Task Force members and Council staff to discuss the report as it evolved. Among these are the American Association of Colleges for Teacher Education, the American Association of School Administrators, the American Public Welfare Association, the American School Health Association, the Association for Supervision and Curriculum Development, the Children's Defense Fund, the Council of Chief State School Officers, the Council of the Great City Schools, the National Association of Elementary School Principals, the National Association of Secondary School Principals, the National Association of State Boards of Education, the National Collaboration for Youth, the National Education Association, the National Middle School Association, the National School Boards Association, and the National Science Teachers Association.

Joseph Foote provided critical help as Editor in completing the report. Anne Lewis assisted in editing, and documented examples of practices we recommend in this report. Kate Wadsworth researched examples of schools and communities already doing what we advocate, along with much of the statistical information appearing in the report. Robert Wiser and Terri Brand designed the imaginative graphics and layout.

We are deeply grateful to the Council staff without whom this report could not have been produced. Ruby Takanishi, Executive Director, provided essential support enabling the Task Force to function effectively, and made many important substantive and editorial contributions to the report. Susan Millstein, Associate Director, provided critical assistance in shaping sections of the report concerning young adolescents' health. Elena Nightingale, Senior Adviser to the Council, and Allyn Mortimer, Program Associate, read and provided thoughtful comments on drafts of the manuscript. Katharine Beckman, Office Manager and Administrative Assistant, adroitly supervised administrative operations. Bronna Clark, Administrative Secretary, assisted in proofreading and provided general support throughout the project. Finally, the Task Force wants especially to acknowledge Annette Dyer, Administrative Secretary, for orchestrating the many details that made the Task Force's effort go smoothly.

Background Paper on Implementing the Task Force's Report on Education of Young Adolescents
Larry Cuban, Stanford University, January 1989.

Forging Effective School-Community Partnerships
Jane Quinn, Girls Clubs of America, November 1988.

Schools in the Center: School, Family, Peer, and Community Connections for More Effective Middle Grades Schools and Students (draft)
Joyce L. Epstein, The Johns Hopkins University, June 1988.

School-Linked Comprehensive Service Delivery Systems
Milbrey W. McLaughlin and Claire Smrekar, Stanford University, June 1988.

The History of the Junior High School: A Study of Conflicting Aims and Institutional Patterns
Daniel Perlstein and William Tobin, Stanford University, June 1988.

Community Service for Young Adolescents
Joan Schine, The City University of New York, June 1988.

Education for Young Adolescents: The Case of Europe and East Asia
Val D. Rust, University of California, Los Angeles, May 1988.

Restructuring Education for Young Adolescents: Possible Guidelines for Local Curriculum Reform
Decker F. Walker, Stanford University, March 1988.

Young Adolescents and Community Service
Joan Schine, The City University of New York, June 1989.

Teaching Decision Making to Adolescents: A Critical Review
Ruth Beyth-Marom, Baruch Fischhoff, Marilyn Jacobs, and Lita Furby, Carnegie-Mellon University and Eugene Research Institute, March 1989.

The Potential of School-Linked Centers to Promote Adolescent Health and Development
Susan G. Millstein, Carnegie Council on Adolescent Development, September 1988.

Adolescent Rolelessness in Modern Society
Elena O. Nightingale and Lisa Wolverton, Carnegie Corporation of New York, September 1988.

Issues in Adolescent Health: An Overview
Karen Hein, Albert Einstein College of Medicine, August 1988.

Preventing Abuse of Drugs, Alcohol, and Tobacco by Adolescents
Mathea Falco, Independent Investigator, June 1988.

AIDS in Adolescence: A Rationale for Concern
Karen Hein, Albert Einstein College of Medicine, June 1988.

APPENDIX C:
CONSULTANTS TO
TASK FORCE MEETINGS

Anthony Cipollone
Senior Research Associate
Education Matters, Inc.
Cambridge, Massachusetts

Janice Earle
Coordinator
Youth Services Program
National Association of State
    Boards of Education
Alexandria, Virginia

Joyce L. Epstein
Program Director
Effective Middle Schools
    Program
Center for Research on
    Elementary and Middle
    Schools
The Johns Hopkins University

Eleanor Farrar
Associate Professor
Educational Organization,
    Administration and Policy
State University of New York
    at Buffalo

Robert Felner
Professor
Department of Psychology
University of Illinois,
    Champagne-Urbana

Hayes Mizell
Director
Program for Disadvantaged
    Youth
The Edna McConnell Clark
    Foundation
New York, New York

Joan Schine
Director
CASE: Early Adolescent Helper
    Program
The City University of New York
    Graduate Center

APPENDIX D:
WORKSHOPS OF THE TASK
FORCE ON EDUCATION OF
YOUNG ADOLESCENTS

**Health Services and
Health Education in
Middle Grade Schools**
June 7–8, 1988
Washington, D.C.

Co-Chairs
    Lawrence W. Green
    Vice President
    Henry J. Kaiser Family
        Foundation
    Menlo Park, California

    Renee R. Jenkins
    Associate Professor of
        Pediatrics
    Director of Adolescent
        Medicine
    Howard University School of
        Medicine
    Washington, D.C.

Kathy Armstrong
Coordinator, Children and
    School Health Programs
Office of Disease Prevention and
    Health Promotion
Washington, D.C.

Denise Dougherty
Project Director, Health
    Program
Office of Technology Assessment
Washington, D.C.

Jill Eden
Analyst, Health Program
Office of Technology Assessment
Washington, D.C.

Beverly K. Farquhar
Executive Director
National Association of School
    Nurses
Scarborough, Maine

Mary Jane Gallagher
Consultant
Gallagher-Widmeyer Group
Washington, D.C.

Beatrix A. Hamburg
Director, Division of Child and
    Adolescent Psychiatry
Mount Sinai School of Medicine
New York, New York

Lloyd Kolbe
Chief of Office of School Health
    and Special Projects
Centers for Disease Control
Atlanta, Georgia

James Lawry
General Practice and Pediatrics
San Francisco, California

Maxine Orey
Director of Adolescent Services
Jackson-Hinds Comprehensive
    Health Center
Jackson, Mississippi

Gary Peck
Director of Ambulatory Care
Louisiana State University
Baton Rouge, Louisiana

Cheryl Perry
Associate Professor
Division of Epidemiology
University of Minnesota
Minneapolis, Minnesota

Anne C. Petersen
Dean, College of Health and
    Human Development
Pennsylvania State University
University Park, Pennsylvania

Jane Quinn
Director, Program Services
Girls Clubs of America
New York, New York

Julius B. Richmond
Professor of Health Policy,
    Emeritus
Division of Health Policy
    Research and Education
Harvard University
Boston, Massachusetts

Ruth Steele
Director
Arkansas State Department of
    Education
Little Rock, Arkansas

Edward Tetelman
Assistant Commissioner
New Jersey Department of
    Human Services
Trenton, New Jersey

Lorraine Tiezzi
Center for Population and Family
    Health
Columbia University
New York, New York

Mary Vernon
Director, Disease Prevention
    Program
Lincoln Community Health
    Center
Durham, North Carolina

Wanda Wesson
Senior Program Specialist
Support Center for School-Based
    Clinics
Houston, Texas

Scott Widmeyer
Consultant
Gallagher-Widmeyer Group
Washington, D.C.

Preparing Teachers for
Middle Grade Schools
September 23, 1988
New York, New York

Chair
    Fred M. Hechinger
    President
    New York Times Company
        Foundation, Inc.
    New York, New York

James P. Comer
Maurice Falk Professor of Child
    Psychiatry
Child Study Center
Yale University
New Haven, Connecticut

David W. Hornbeck
Of Counsel, Hogan and Hartson
Visiting Professor of Education
  and Public Policy
The Johns Hopkins University
Baltimore, Maryland

David Mandel
Vice President for Policy
  Development
National Board for Professional
  Teaching Standards
Washington, D.C.

Deborah W. Meier
Principal
Central Park East **Secondary**
  School
New York, New York

Lorraine Monroe
Director, Center for Minority
  Achievement
Bank Street College
New York, New York

*Developing An Impact Strategy
for the Task Force Report*
September 30, 1988
Washington, D.C.

Chair
  David W. Hornbeck
  Of Counsel, Hogan and
    Hartson
  Visiting Professor of
    Education and Public Policy
  The Johns Hopkins University
  Baltimore, Maryland

Fred M. Hechinger
President
New York Times Company
  Foundation, Inc.
New York, New York

Hernan LaFontaine
Superintendent
Hartford Public Schools
Hartford, Connecticut

Anne Lewis
Writer
Task Force on Education of
  Young Adolescents
Washington, D.C.

Jane Quinn
Director, Program Services
Girls Clubs of America
New York, New York

Julius B. Richmond
Professor of Health Policy,
  Emeritus
Division of Health Policy
  Research and Education
Harvard University
Boston, Massachusetts

Marshall S. Smith
Dean, School of Education
Stanford University
Stanford, California

Wilma Tisch
New York, New York

Marla Ucelli
Special Assistant to the
  Governor for Education
State of New Jersey
Trenton, New Jersey

Scott Widmeyer
Consultant
Gallagher-Widmeyer Group
Washington, D.C.

*Implementation of Task Force
Recommendations*
January 23, 1989
Washington, D.C.

Chair
  David W. Hornbeck
  Of Counsel, Hogan and
    Hartson
  Visiting Professor of
    Education and Public Policy
  The Johns Hopkins University
  Baltimore, Maryland

Barbara Bazron
Executive Director
Pittsburgh New Futures, Inc.
Pittsburgh, Pennsylvania

Alonzo A. Crim
Benjamin E. Mays Chair of
    Urban Educational Leadership
Department of Educational
    Administration
Georgia State University
Atlanta, Georgia

Janice Earle
Coordinator, Youth Services
    Program
National Association of State
    Boards of Education
Alexandria, Virginia

Judith Meyers
Policy Analyst
Governor's Office of Human
    Resources
The Commonwealth of
    Massachusetts
Boston, Massachusetts

Hayes Mizell
Director
Program for Disadvantaged
    Youth
The Edna McConnell Clark
    Foundation
New York, New York

Ann Rosewater
Staff Director
Select Committee on Children,
    Youth and Families
Washington, D.C.

Phillip Schlechty
President
Center for Leadership in School
    Reform
Louisville, Kentucky

Fred Tempes
Assistant Superintendent
Instructional Support Service
    Division
California State Department of
    Education
Sacramento, California

Marla Ucelli
Special Assistant to the
    Governor for Education
State of New Jersey
Trenton, New Jersey

Consultation with California Foundation Schools Principals
February 1, 1989
San Diego, California

Duff Danilovich
Principal
Los Cerros Intermediate School
Danville, California

William Demos
Principal
Montgomery Junior High School
San Diego, California

Thaddeus Dumas
Office of Middle Grades Support
    Services
State Department of Education
Sacramento, California

James Fenwick
Fenwick Associates
San Diego, California

Evelyn Hodel
Principal
Woodlake Intermediate School
Woodlake, California

Marianne Overton
Office of Middle Grades Support
    Services
State Department of Education
Sacramento, California

Alan Rasmussen
Principal
Dwyer Middle School
Huntington Beach, California

Robert Schallig
Office of Middle Grades Support
  Services
State Department of Education
Sacramento, California

Don Simpson
Principal
Shandin Hills Intermediate
  School
San Bernadino, California

Roger Skinner
Principal
Chaparral Middle School
Diamond Bar, California

Jana K. Slater
Special Studies and Evaluation
  Reports Office
Office of Middle Grades Support
  Services
State Department of Education
Sacramento, California

Penni Todd
Office of Middle Grades Support
  Services
State Department of Education
Sacramento, California

Michael D. Trenton
Principal
Central Middle School
Oroville, California

Robert Welch
Principal
Burlingame Intermediate School
Burlingame, California

David Wildman
Principal
Silverado Middle School
Napa, California

Edna Wilson
Principal
Bret Harte Preparatory
  Intermediate School
Los Angeles, California

David W. Hornbeck
Chair, Task Force on Education of Young Adolescents

After 12 years as State Superintendent of Schools for Maryland, David W. Hornbeck joined the Washington firm of Hogan and Hartson in 1988. He is also Visiting Professor of Education and Public Policy at The Johns Hopkins University. His experience and interest in public policymaking for children and youth is evidenced in a number of leadership roles. Mr. Hornbeck is Chair of the Board of Trustees for the Carnegie Foundation for the Advancement of Teaching; a member of the board for the Children's Defense Fund and the National Christina Foundation; a member of the William T. Grant Foundation Commission on Work, Family and Citizenship; a member of the education committee of the United States Committee for UNICEF; and Chair of the advisory committee on the Program for Disadvantaged Youth of the Edna McConnell Clark Foundation. He is a former President of the Council of Chief State School Officers and served as Executive Deputy Secretary of Education for the Commonwealth of Pennsylvania before moving to Maryland. Mr. Hornbeck received a B.A. degree from Austin College, a diploma in theology from Oxford University, a B.D. degree from Union Theological Seminary, and a J.D. degree from the University of Pennsylvania.

Bill Clinton

Bill Clinton is the 42nd Governor of Arkansas, an office to which he has been re-elected three times. He has used his gubernatorial leadership to bring about dramatic reforms in education, both at the state and national levels. He campaigned successfully for higher standards in the public schools in Arkansas and increased taxes to support them. His most recent initiative for children has been to improve state health services. Governor Clinton is a past chairman of the Education Commission of the States and the author of its comprehensive report on the importance of leadership for education reform, *Speaking of Leadership*. As chairman of the National Governors' Association (NGA), Governor Clinton led a major effort to reform federal welfare policy that was approved by Congress in 1988. He currently serves as chairman of NGA's Task Force on Children and as chairman of the Democratic Governors' Association. Governor Clinton has a B.A. degree from Georgetown University, attended Oxford University as a Rhodes Scholar, and received his law degree from Yale University.

James P. Comer

James P. Comer is Maurice Falk Professor of Child Psychiatry at the Yale University Child Study Center and director of the Center's School Development Program. His interest in the changing conditions surrounding child-rearing in this country, particularly of Black children, led to his work on preventive strategies for low-income children in elementary schools. A successful intervention program initially developed in the New Haven, Connecticut, schools is now being implemented in several other states and was the subject of one of Dr. Comer's books, *School Power: Implications of an Intervention Project*. Dr. Comer is a columnist for

Parents Magazine, as well as a consultant for the Children's Television Workshop and Associate Dean of the Yale University School of Medicine. He describes his own family and educational experiences in his 1988 book, *Maggie's American Dream*. Dr. Comer received an A.B. degree from Indiana University, an M.D. degree from Howard University, and an M.P.H. from the University of Michigan.

Alonzo A. Crim

Alonzo A. Crim holds the Benjamin E. Mays Chair of Urban Educational Leadership in the Department of Educational Administration at Georgia State University. As Superintendent of the Atlanta, Georgia, public schools for 15 years, Dr. Crim introduced many innovative programs in the predominantly Black and low-income Atlanta school district that resulted in a dramatic increase in the number of students completing high school and continuing to post-secondary education. One of these innovations was a district-wide requirement of community service for a high school diploma. A frequently honored educator, Dr. Crim began his career as a 7th and 8th grade science and mathematics teacher. He later served as a Principal and District Superintendent in Chicago and Superintendent of the Compton, California, Unified School District. Dr. Crim received a B.A. degree in sociology from Roosevelt College in Chicago, an M.A. in educational administration from the University of Chicago, and an Ed.D from the Harvard Graduate School of Education.

Jacquelynne Eccles

Jacquelynne Eccles is Professor of Psychology at the University of Colorado and Research Scientist at the Institute for Social Research at the University of Michigan. Since 1978, she has been involved in numerous research projects on the transition experiences of young adolescents from elementary to junior high school environments and related issues, such as school anxiety, family support, and gender development. With grants from the National Institute of Child Health and Human Development, Dr. Eccles is the principal researcher for a longitudinal study that is following more than 2,500 students from 5th grade through high school. She is the recipient of a Spencer Award from the National Academy of Education and is a Fellow of the Society for the Psychological Study of Social Issues. Dr. Eccles was a member of the faculty and Assistant Vice President for Research at the University of Michigan; she began her career as a science and mathematics teacher at the junior and senior high school level. She received a B.A. from the University of California at Berkeley and a Ph.D. in psychology from the University of California at Los Angeles.

Lawrence W. Green

Lawrence W. Green became Vice President and Director of the Health Promotion Program of the Henry J. Kaiser Family Foundation in 1988 after many years as a researcher, administrator, and public official in the field of health promotion. He founded the Center for Health Promotion Research and Development at the University of Texas Medical School at Houston. He also has served on the public health faculties of the University of California at Berkeley, Harvard University, and The Johns

Hopkins University, where he established the graduate programs in health education and was Head of the Division of Health Education. During the Carter Administration, Dr. Green was Director of the Office of Health Information, Health Promotion, Physical Fitness, and Sports Medicine. He is a past President of the Society for Public Health Education and author of four books on health promotion and serves on the editorial boards of several journals in the health sciences. Dr. Green received B.S., M.P.H., and Dr.P.H. degrees from the University of California at Berkeley.

Fred M. Hechinger

Fred M. Hechinger is President of the New York Times Company Foundation, Inc. An education columnist for the *New York Times*, he was the education editor of that newspaper from 1959 to 1969 and a member of the Editorial Board before heading the Foundation. Mr. Hechinger has authored or co-authored with his wife, Grace, a number of books about American education and youth, including *A Better Start* and *Growing Up in America.* He is a former education editor of *Parents' Magazine* and also a former President of the Education Writers Association, from which he has received a number of awards for his writing about education. Mr. Hechinger has received the George Polk Memorial Award, and he holds the British Empire Medal. He is a member of the board of Carnegie Corporation, the Academy for Educational Development, and the Foreign Policy Association. Mr. Hechinger is a graduate of The City College of New York.

Renee R. Jenkins

Renee R. Jenkins is Associate Professor of Pediatrics in the Department of Pediatrics and Child Health at the Howard University College of Medicine, where she also is Director of Adolescent Medicine. At Howard University, Dr. Jenkins was the first Director of Adolescent Services, a program that includes a service unit in the hospital, ambulatory clinics and community outreach services for adolescents. Dr. Jenkins serves as the President of the Society for Adolescent Medicine. She also is Chair of the Mayor's Advisory Panel on Teen Pregnancy Prevention in Washington, D.C. Dr. Jenkins served on the Committee on Adolescence of the American Academy of Pediatrics for seven years and currently serves on its Committee on Community Health Services. A graduate of Wayne State University School of Medicine, she completed her residency and fellowship training at Albert Einstein/Jacobi Hospital programs in New York City.

Nancy Landon Kassebaum

Nancy Landon Kassebaum has been a Member of the United States Senate from Kansas since 1978. Senator Kassebaum grew up in a political environment as the daughter of Alfred Landon, Governor of Kansas and 1936 Republican presidential nominee. She is the Ranking Minority Member of the Senate Subcommittee on Education, Arts, and Humanities and former Chairperson, now Ranking Minority Member, of the Subcommittee on African Affairs of the Committee on Foreign Relations. Senator Kassebaum also served on the Committee on Banking, Housing and Urban Affairs and the Special Committee on Aging. She is Honorary

Chairman of the Commission on the Future of Community Colleges and a member of the U.S.-Mexico Commission. Senator Kassebaum received a B.A. degree from the University of Kansas and an M.A. degree in diplomatic history from the University of Michigan.

Hernan LaFontaine

Superintendent of the Hartford, Connecticut, public schools since 1979, Hernan LaFontaine was an early leader in the move for quality bilingual education programs in the public schools. He established the first completely bilingual school in the New York City school system in 1968, then became head of a newly established Office of Bilingual Education for the entire system. He began his education career as a science teacher in a Bronx junior high school and served also as an Assistant Principal of an intermediate school in Manhattan. Mr. LaFontaine is a member of the Policy Committee of the National Assessment of Educational Progress, the board of directors of the National Council of La Raza, and the American Leadership Forum. He is a past President of the Connecticut Association of Urban Superintendents. Mr. LaFontaine received his B.S. and M.A. degrees from The City College of New York.

Deborah W. Meier

Deborah W. Meier is the Principal of Central Park East Secondary School in New York City's East Harlem. Beginning in 1974, Ms. Meier has been instrumental in creating three alternative public elementary schools in the city's District 4. In 1985 she helped create the Central Park East Secondary School, which includes grades 7 to 12. The schools under Ms. Meier's stewardship were cited as "among the best in New York City" by the John D. and Catherine T. MacArthur Foundation when it selected her as the first teacher for a foundation award in 1987. She taught in the public schools of Chicago and Philadelphia before coming to New York City and was a teacher educator before becoming a Principal. Ms. Meier is a member of the National Board for Professional Teaching Standards. She also is a founding member of the North Dakota Study Group on Assessment. She received a B.A. degree from Antioch College and an M.A. in American history from the University of Chicago.

Amado M. Padilla

Amado M. Padilla is Professor of Education in the School of Education at Stanford University, where he also is a member of the Stanford University Center for the Study of Families, Children and Youth. He previously was Director and Principal Investigator of the Center for Language Education and Research at the University of California at Los Angeles. Dr. Padilla's research interests include early childhood bilingualism and the social adaptation of immigrants and their children to American society. He is a member of the Committee on Child Development Research and Public Policy of the National Research Council, and formerly directed the National Center for Bilingual Research at Los Alamitos, California, and the Spanish-Speaking Mental Health Research Center at the University of California at Los Angeles. Dr. Padilla has received numerous awards and published extensively in the area of bilingualism and Hispanic mental health issues. He received a B.A. degree from New Mexico Highlands University, an M.S. degree in experimental psychology from Oklahoma State University, and a Ph.D. in experimental psychology from the University of New Mexico.

Anne C. Petersen

Anne C. Petersen is Dean of the College of Health and Human Development at Pennsylvania State University. Her professional career as a researcher and author has centered on adolescent development, particularly in regard to gender differences. She currently is a consultant to the Robert Wood Johnson Foundation on the evaluation of school-based adolescent health care and to the John D. and Catherine T. MacArthur Foundation on health issues, and is on the editorial board of the *Journal of Early Adolescence.* Dr. Petersen formerly served as Coordinator of the clinical research training program in adolescence at the Michael Reese Hospital and Medical Center and as Director of its Laboratory for the Study of Adolescence. She also is a member of committees concerned with children and families of the Social Science Research Council and the National Academy of Sciences' Institute of Medicine. Dr. Petersen received B.A., M.S., and Ph.D. degrees from the University of Chicago in mathematics and statistical analysis.

Jane M. Quinn

As Director of Program Services for Girls Clubs of America, Jane M. Quinn is responsible for program services and program development for 240 Girls Clubs throughout the country. During her eight years with the national office, Ms. Quinn has directed development of national programs in adolescent pregnancy prevention, health promotion, substance abuse prevention, child abuse prevention, computer literacy, sports, and youth employment. A clinical social worker, she was involved in casework and supervision of health programs for mothers and children for the District of Columbia Department of Human Resources and directed a technical assistance program to help youth-serving agencies expand their sexuality education for the Center for Population Options. Ms. Quinn received a B.A. degree from the College of New Rochelle and an M.A. from the University of Chicago.

Mary Budd Rowe

Mary Budd Rowe is Professor of Science Education at the University of Florida. Currently, she is editor of the research section for several journals concerned with science education, science consultant to the television series *Reading Rainbow,* a member of the advisory board for the science television series *3-2-1 Contact,* and a member of the subcommittee on minorities in engineering of the National Academy of Sciences. Dr. Rowe is the immediate past President of the National Science Teachers Association. She also is a member of the National Board for Professional Teaching Standards and a consultant to school districts in the United States and abroad on their science programs. Dr. Rowe has received several prestigious awards for her work in research about and development of science curricula. She holds a B.A. degree from New Jersey State

University at Montclair, an M.A. in zoology from the University of California at Berkeley, and a Ph.D in science education from Stanford University.

Roberta G. Simmons

Roberta G. Simmons, Professor of Psychiatry and Sociology at the University of Pittsburgh, has written extensively on school transitions, sex roles, and self-esteem among young adolescents. She is a past recipient of a Guggenheim Fellowship and of awards from the National Institute of Mental Health Research. In the fall of 1986, she was a Fellow at the Center for Advanced Study in Behavioral Sciences in Palo Alto, California. She is a Fellow of the American Association for the Advancement of Science. Dr. Simmons is co-author of *Moving into Adolescence: The Impact of Pubertal Change and School Context.* She is a consulting editor of *Child Development,* a member of the Council for the Society for Research on Adolescence, President of the Midwest Sociological Society, and Vice-President of the Eastern Sociological Association. Dr. Simmons received a B.A. degree from Wellesley College and M.A. and Ph.D degrees in sociology from Columbia University.

Marshall S. Smith

Marshall S. Smith is Dean of the School of Education at Stanford University and a past Director of the Wisconsin Center for Education Research at the University of Wisconsin at Madison. His research and professional experiences center on education policy. Dr. Smith is a member of the Commission on Behavioral and Social Sciences and Education of the National Research Council, a member of the Advisory Committee for Science and Engineering Education of the National Science Foundation, a board member of the National Health Policy Forum, and a member of the Cleveland Conference. He was a co-author of *Inequality: A Reassessment of the Effect of Family and Schooling in America* and has written extensively on federal policy in education. Dr. Smith received an A.B. degree from Harvard College and a Ph.D. in measurement and statistics from the Harvard Graduate School of Education.

COMING SOON

from

Teachers College Press

Turning Points 2000:
Educating Adolescents in the 21st Century

by Anthony W. Jackson and Gayle A. Davis

Ten years after the landmark Carnegie Corporation report *Turning Points: Preparing American Youth for the 21st Century,* we are proud to announce the forthcoming publication of *Turning Points 2000: Educating Adolescents in the 21st Century.* Based on the experiences of hundreds of schools and the most current research, the book provides in-depth information on implementing the Turning Points principles of middle school education. *Turning Points 2000* is thorough in its overview of improving education for young adolescents and will thus be indispensable to teachers, administrators, researchers, parents, community groups, and others interested in school reform. Publication is scheduled for the fall of 2000.

For information, please contact:

Teachers College Press
1234 Amsterdam Avenue
New York, New York 10027
(212) 678-3929